Katrin Cargill's

simple curtains

creative ideas & 20 step-by-step projects

Katrin Cargill's
simple curtains

creative ideas & 20 step-by-step projects

Katrin Cargill
photography by James Merrell

RYLAND
PETERS
& SMALL
LONDON NEW YORK

For this edition:
Designers Saskia Janssen and
    Sarah Fraser
Editor Miriam Hyslop
Production Sheila Smith
Art Director Gabriella Le Grazie
Publishing Director Alison Starling
Illustrator Michael Hill

First published in Great Britain in 1998
and reissued with amendments in 2005
by Ryland Peters & Small
20–21 Jockey's Fields
London WC1R 4BW
www.rylandpeters.com

Printed in China

ISBN 1 84172 793 8

A catalogue record for this book is
available from the British Library

Contents

introduction 6
use of fabrics 8
yellow checks 10
horizontal stripes 14
two-way striped voile 18
appliqué scrolls 22
contrast-bordered linen 26

headings 30
reversible scallops 32
button-on silk 36
concertina stripes 40
tie-on muslin sheers 44

valances and pelmets 48
gathered gingham 50
monogrammed linen valance 54
beaded zigzags 58

red-trimmed voile 62
shaped linen valance 66
rope-edged valance 70
gypsy-skirted valance 74

edgings 78
italian stringing with bow 80
squares on squares 84
contrast-scalloped border 88
pictorial-edged curtains 92

equipment and techniques 96
templates 102
directory of suppliers 106
credits 108
glossary 110
index 111
acknowledgments 112

In recent years there has been a revolution in the world of curtains. Grandeur and formality have been replaced with simplicity and freshness — enormous swags and tails made from acres of brocade, over-ornate pelmets and flouncy festoon blinds have given way to clean lines, subtle textures and strong colours. This impetus towards a mood of simple, effortless elegance has resulted in a new freedom when it comes to making curtains. Simple curtains make stylish statements that are subtly effective rather than overly dramatic. They will enliven and enhance any window without dominating it. Because they do not require metres and metres of material, you can use that irresistible fabric without breaking the bank and blowing your budget.

For this book, I have searched out simple curtain ideas that are practical and uncomplicated and well-suited to the windows they have been made for. So often, one sees a terrific pair of curtains on completely the wrong window. Try to be sensitive to the dimensions of the window and the proportions of the room. There are fewer rules than ever before for lengths and widths of curtains, so I have tried to show as many examples as possible of treatments that work because they are sensitive to scale. I hope that this book will inspire you to simplify and unclutter your windows!

Katrin Cargill

use of fabrics

Fabric comes in a wide and dazzling array of colours, textures and patterns. By piecing together fabric in unexpected combinations, you will achieve innovative and original effects. Be adventurous, and experiment with contrasting textures and different designs, all cunningly combined in a single pair of curtains. Creative and imaginative use of fabrics will enable you to make elegant, stylish and totally unique curtains.

below *An inexpensive slubby cotton has been lined and interlined for a luxurious and opulent effect. The bobbled border at the top of the curtains creates textural interest.*
below left *Black-and-white antique Toile de Jouy curtains are teamed with an irreverent red bobble fringing to create a timeless look at an elegant window. Unexpected combinations like this will enliven a simple pair of curtains.*

left *A stylish alternative to the ubiquitous white nets. A checked red-and-white voile serves the same purpose — privacy — but with a little more verve and colour.*

below far left *Ready-made tab-topped curtains are dyed in oranges, yellows and reds. The fabric filters light and creates a dappled effect.*

below centre left *Two pairs of curtains on separate poles, one made from flimsy muslin and the other cotton moiré, create an interesting layered look.*

below centre right *The narrow edging on these pretty Toile de Jouy curtains brings definition to the leading edge and frames an unusual round window. An upholstered slipper chair has been covered in the same fabric and continues the feminine yet unfussy theme.*

below far right *Crisp white cotton allows light to filter into a room, yet provides both privacy and shade.*

yellow checks

These cheerful, colourful yellow curtains are guaranteed to bring a relaxed, sunny atmosphere to any room, even in the darkest depths of winter. They use panels of three coordinating fabrics joined horizontally. A vivid scarlet braid is sewn over the seams to conceal any unsightly joins on the front of the curtain. The bold checks and braid have a pleasing rustic simplicity that is echoed by the simple ties that hold the curtains to an iron pole.

materials & equipment

three different main fabrics

lining fabric

1.5 cm (⅝ in) wide red braid

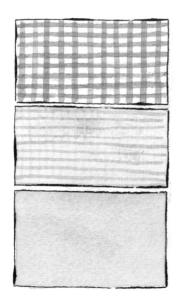

1 Measure the window to calculate fabric quantities (see Techniques, page 96). Each panel occupies one third of the drop of the finished curtain. Add 1.5 cm (⅝ in) to each panel for each seam. Add 8 cm (3 in) to the top panel for the heading and 16 cm (6½ in) to the bottom panel for the hem. Each curtain must be the width of the pole plus 12 cm (4¾ in) for side hems. The lining must be 4 cm (1¾ in) smaller than the finished curtain all round. Cut out the fabric.

2 Place the top panel on a flat surface with the middle panel on top, right sides together and raw edges aligned. Pin, baste and machine stitch the two panels together, using a 1.5 cm (⅝ in) seam allowance and matching up the checks as best you can. Press open the seam. Attach the bottom panel to the middle panel in the same way.

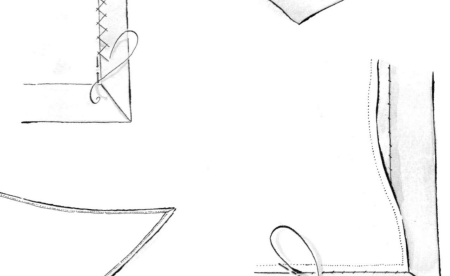

3 Cut two strips of braid to the width of the curtain. Centre the braid over the seams between the panels on the right side of the curtain. Pin, baste and machine stitch down both edges of the braid.

4 Press in a 6 cm (2½ in) hem at each side of the curtain and a double 8 cm (3 in) hem at the bottom. Press in the angled mitres (see Techniques, page 100). Pin and baste the hems in place. Herringbone stitch the side hems. Slip stitch the base hem and the mitres.

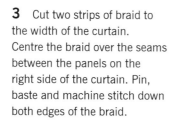

5 Cut out the lining. Press in a 2 cm (¾ in) hem along each side edge and a 2 cm (¾ in) double base hem. Pin and baste the hems. Mitre the corners (see Techniques, page 100) and machine stitch the hems in place.

6 Place the curtain on a flat surface, wrong side up. Place the lining on top, right side up. Match up the corners of the lining with the mitred corners of the curtain and align the top raw edges. Pin the curtain and lining together along the top raw edges. Pin and baste the lining to the curtain. Slip stitch the lining to the curtain fabric. Leave the bottom of the lining open, as the curtain will hang better.

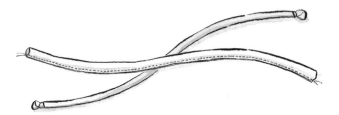

7 The number of ties needed will depend on the width of the curtain. There should be one tie every 25 cm (10 in). Cut a strip of fabric, 6 x 50 cm (2½ x 20 in), for each tie. Make up the ties (see Techniques, page 101), knotting the ends of each one.

8 Lay the curtain flat, right side up. Using fabric pen, lightly mark a line 8 cm (3 in) below the top raw edge. Place a tie at each top corner of the curtain and space the other ties at 25 cm (10 in) intervals in between. Pin and baste the halfway point of each tie to the marked line, then machine stitch all the way along the line, taking in the ties as you go.

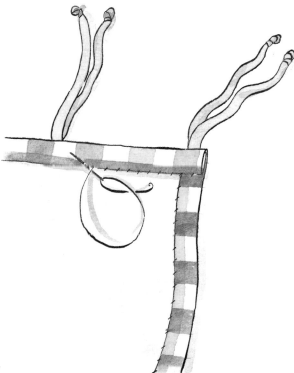

9 Press in a double 4 cm (1¾ in) fold to the wrong side along the top edges of the curtain. Pin, baste and slip stitch the folded edge of the curtain to the lining.

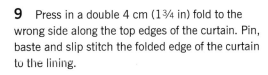

10 Working at the two top corners of the curtain, slip stitch the open ends of the top hem together. Press the finished curtains, then tie them to the pole with loose bows.

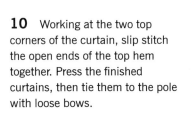

horizontal stripes

These elegant, formal curtains flank a window recess and are not intended to be drawn. The heavy horizontal stripes in sombre shades have a stately, classical grandeur, and the curtains are lined and interlined for an opulent, luxurious effect. Despite the bold stripes, the curtains are extremely simple and do not detract from the antique wooden pole, gleaming polished finials and ornate brass bosses in the shape of a flower.

materials & equipment

cotton fabric

contrasting cotton fabric

interlining

lining fabric

9 cm (3 ½ in) wide pinch pleat heading tape

curtain hooks

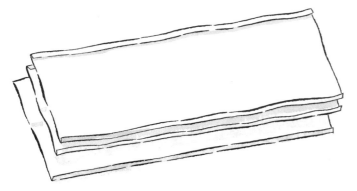

1 To calculate how much fabric you will need, measure the window (see Techniques, page 96). These curtains have a pinch pleat heading, so require fabric two and a half times the width of the pole. However, they are not designed to be drawn, so halve the width of the pole then calculate the fabric quantities accordingly. Add 16 cm (6½ in) to the length for hem and heading and 12 cm (4¾ in) to the width for side hems.

2 The interlining must be the same size as the curtain without hem allowances and the lining must be 4 cm (1¾ in) smaller than the finished curtain all round. Cut out the fabric, lining and interlining. Join widths if necessary (see Techniques, page 98). For the stripes, cut three panels of fabric to the width of the curtain, each panel one sixth of the length of the curtain. Add 3 cm (1¼ in) seam allowance to the length of each panel and another 8 cm (3 in) to the top panel. Press a 1.5 cm (⅝ in) fold along both the long edges of the two smaller bands. On the larger strip press in just one fold.

3 Place the largest panel at the top of the curtain and position the other two beneath it at regular intervals. Pin, baste and machine stitch the panels, right side up, to the right side of the main curtain fabric, lining up the side edges.

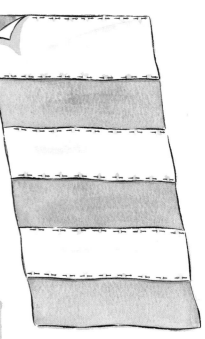

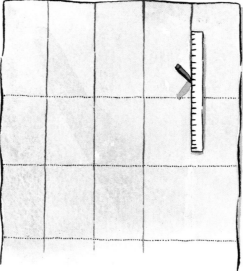

4 Place the curtain right side down. Use a ruler and fabric pen to mark a series of vertical lines, each 30 cm (12 in) apart, on the wrong side of the fabric across the entire curtain width.

5 Place the curtain on a flat surface, right side down, and position the interlining on top, 8 cm (3 in) beneath the top edge of the curtain and 6 cm (2½ in) in from each side. Fold back the interlining lengthways until the fold aligns with the first line, then lock stitch the interlining to the curtain, working from bottom to top (see Techniques, page 99). Continue in this way until the interlining is locked in across the width of the curtain.

6 At each side of the curtain, press in a 6 cm (2½ in) fold over the interlining. Then fold up an 8 cm (3 in) single hem at the bottom edge and press in place. Fold and press in the angled mitres at the bottom corners of the curtain (see Techniques, page 100).

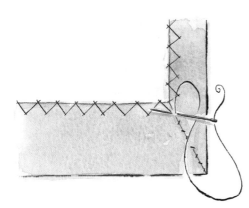

7 Pin and baste the hems in place. Herringbone stitch the side and base hems and slip stitch the mitres.

8 Place the lining right side down on a flat surface. Press in a 2 cm (¾ in) fold down each side edge of the lining and a double 2 cm (¾ in) hem along the bottom edge. Mitre the corners and press. Pin, baste and machine stitch the side and bottom hems in place.

9 Place the curtain on a flat surface, interlined side up. Place the lining on top, right side up. Match up the corners of the lining with the mitred corners of the main fabric and align the top raw edges. Pin the curtain and lining together along their top edges, making sure that the material lies completely flat. Baste then slip stitch the edges of the lining to the curtain. Leave the bottom of the lining open as the curtain will hang better.

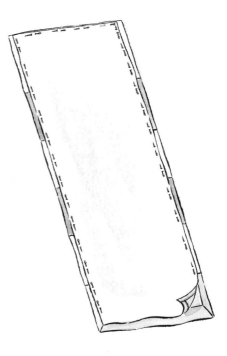

10 Cut the heading tape to the width of the curtain plus 3 cm (1¼ in) at each end. Knot the strings at the leading edge and leave them loose at the other. At the top of the curtain press over an 8 cm (3 in) fold to the wrong side. Pin the tape over the fold, 1 cm (½ in) below the edge, tucking in the raw ends. Pin, baste and machine stitch the tape in place. Pull the strings and knot the end. Insert the hooks and hang the curtain.

two-way striped voile

Here, in a simple arrangement requiring little sewing, striped voile curtains are suspended from metal eyelets punched through the fabric and hung from hooks screwed above the window. The curtains can either hang loose or be knotted out of the way. The stripes have been turned to the horizontal to create a smart contrasting heading strip.

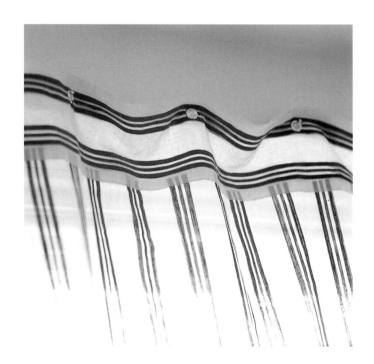

materials & equipment

striped voile fabric

metal eyelets

hole punch kit

hooks

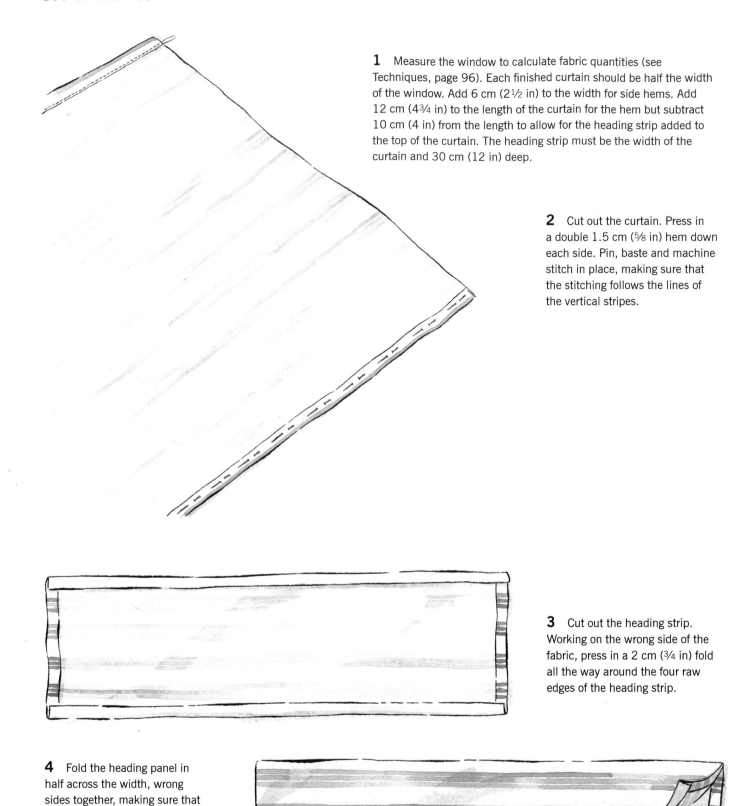

1 Measure the window to calculate fabric quantities (see Techniques, page 96). Each finished curtain should be half the width of the window. Add 6 cm (2½ in) to the width for side hems. Add 12 cm (4¾ in) to the length of the curtain for the hem but subtract 10 cm (4 in) from the length to allow for the heading strip added to the top of the curtain. The heading strip must be the width of the curtain and 30 cm (12 in) deep.

2 Cut out the curtain. Press in a double 1.5 cm (⅝ in) hem down each side. Pin, baste and machine stitch in place, making sure that the stitching follows the lines of the vertical stripes.

3 Cut out the heading strip. Working on the wrong side of the fabric, press in a 2 cm (¾ in) fold all the way around the four raw edges of the heading strip.

4 Fold the heading panel in half across the width, wrong sides together, making sure that the folded edges meet. Press along the fold.

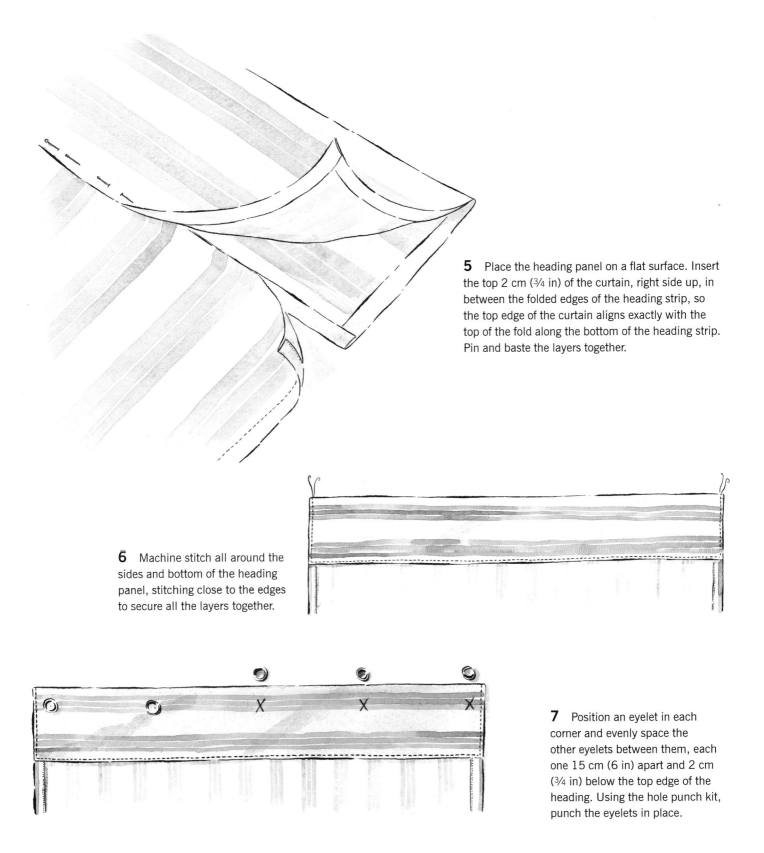

5 Place the heading panel on a flat surface. Insert the top 2 cm (¾ in) of the curtain, right side up, in between the folded edges of the heading strip, so the top edge of the curtain aligns exactly with the top of the fold along the bottom of the heading strip. Pin and baste the layers together.

6 Machine stitch all around the sides and bottom of the heading panel, stitching close to the edges to secure all the layers together.

7 Position an eyelet in each corner and evenly space the other eyelets between them, each one 15 cm (6 in) apart and 2 cm (¾ in) below the top edge of the heading. Using the hole punch kit, punch the eyelets in place.

8 Insert correspondingly positioned screw hooks into the wall or frame above the window and hang the curtain. Mark the hem line with pins. Take down the curtain, and along the bottom edge, press in a double hem to the wrong side.

9 Pin, baste and machine stitch the hem in place, then press and rehang the curtain.

appliqué scrolls

These coarsely textured, cream hessian curtains are appliquéd with a scroll border in a smooth blue chintz. The rhythmic repetition of the scrolls adds definition to the window and the combination of dynamic shapes and bold colours creates a dramatic, almost theatrical effect. These curtains are not suited to small or low-set windows, as they could appear squat and heavy. Instead, reserve them for larger windows or doors, and keep the rest of the decor simple.

materials & equipment

coarse hessian fabric

chintz or cotton fabric for the appliqué border

1 Measure your window to calculate fabric quantities (see Techniques, page 96). Each curtain must be half the width of the window plus 6 cm (2½ in) for side hems. Add 11.5 cm (4½ in) to the length for hem and heading. Each curtain has an appliqué border; an L-shaped piece of fabric the same width and length as the curtain and 45 cm (18 in) deep. Add 1.5 cm (⅝ in) to the depth of the short strip for the heading and 10 cm (4 in) to the length of the long strip for the hem. Each curtain needs a heading strip of appliqué fabric, 6 cm (2½ in) deep and the width of the curtain.

2 Cut out all the fabric. Make a template for the border (see Templates, page 102). Place the border fabric on a flat surface, pin the template to the top panel and mark around the outline of the template all the way along the strip and around the corner. Cut along the marked line.

3 Press in a 1 cm (½ in) fold to the wrong side of the fabric all around the curved edges of the scrolls, clipping the curves so they lie flat.

4 Place the hessian panel right side up on a flat surface and place the border on top, right side up, aligning the straight edges. Pin and baste the two layers together around the outside edges and inside curves of the border. Machine stitch around the curved edges of the scrolls only, working on the right side of the curtain.

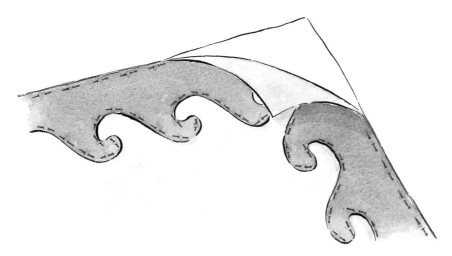

5 Press a 3 cm (1¼ in) hem into the wrong side of the curtain along the long side edges and pin, baste and machine stitch in place. Press a 5 cm (2 in) double hem up along the bottom edge of the curtain. Mitre the corners. Pin, baste and machine stitch in place.

6 Cut strips of fabric for the ties, each one measuring 10 x 75 cm (4 x 30 in). Turn in a 5 mm (¼ in) fold all the way around the edges of the strips and press. Pin, baste and machine stitch the hems. Fold each completed tie in half, wrong sides together, and press.

7 Place the curtain right side up on a flat surface. Position the ties along the top of the curtain, the folded edge of each tie aligned with the top raw edge of the curtain. Pin and baste the ties in place across their pressed halfway mark.

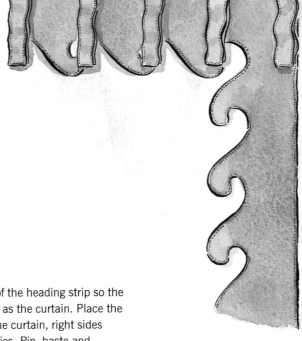

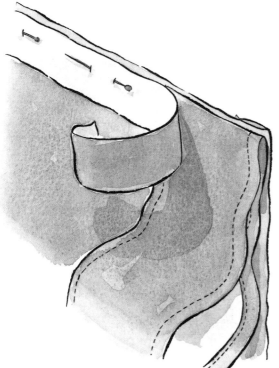

8 Press in the ends of the heading strip so the strip is the same width as the curtain. Place the strip along the top of the curtain, right sides together, covering the ties. Pin, baste and machine stitch along the top raw edge of the curtain, using a 1.5 cm (⅝ in) seam allowance.

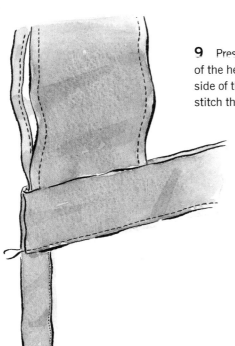

9 Press in a 1.5 cm (⅝ in) fold along the raw edge of the heading strip. Fold the strip over to the wrong side of the curtain, then pin, baste and machine stitch the folded edge to the back of the curtain.

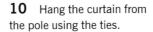

10 Hang the curtain from the pole using the ties.

contrast-bordered linen

These classic pencil pleat curtains have an unexpected feature — a deep border at the hem, in the same fabric but in a contrasting colour, which just rests upon the ground. Adding contrast borders is a simple yet effective device, for they bring colour and contrast to the plainest of curtains and add interest to a neutral, understated colour scheme.

materials & equipment

main fabric

contrasting fabric for the border

lining fabric

8 cm (3 in) wide pencil pleat heading tape

curtain hooks

1 To work out how much fabric you will need, measure your window (see Techniques, page 96). These curtains have a pencil pleat heading, which requires material two and a half to three times the width of the pole or track. Add 12 cm (4¾ in) to the width for the side hems. The length of the main material is five-sixths of the drop from pole to floor. Add 8 cm (3 in) for the heading, and 1.5 cm (⅝ in) seam allowance to attach the contrasting border.

2 The contrasting material for the border must be the same width as the main curtain plus 12 cm (4¾ in) for the side hems. The length of the border should be one sixth of the drop from pole to floor. Add 16 cm (6½ in) for the hem, and 1.5 cm (⅝ in) seam allowance at the top to attach the border to the main material.

3 Cut out the main fabric and the contrasting border fabric. Join widths as necessary (see Techniques, page 98).

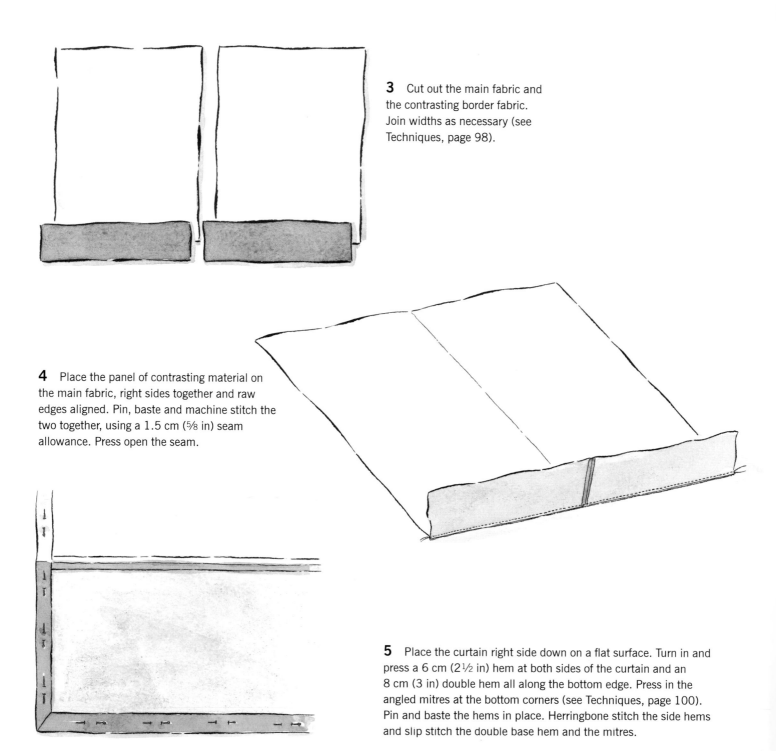

4 Place the panel of contrasting material on the main fabric, right sides together and raw edges aligned. Pin, baste and machine stitch the two together, using a 1.5 cm (⅝ in) seam allowance. Press open the seam.

5 Place the curtain right side down on a flat surface. Turn in and press a 6 cm (2½ in) hem at both sides of the curtain and an 8 cm (3 in) double hem all along the bottom edge. Press in the angled mitres at the bottom corners (see Techniques, page 100). Pin and baste the hems in place. Herringbone stitch the side hems and slip stitch the double base hem and the mitres.

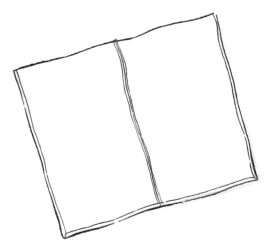

6 The lining fabric should be 4 cm (1¾ in) smaller all round than the finished curtain. Cut out the lining fabric and join widths if necessary (see Techniques, page 98). Turn in and press a 2 cm (¾ in) hem along each side edge of the lining and a double 2 cm (¾ in) hem along the bottom edge. Mitre the corners and press. Pin, baste and machine stitch the side and bottom hems in place.

7 Place the curtain on a flat surface, wrong side up. Place the lining on top of the curtain, right side up. Match up the corners of the lining with the mitred corners of the curtain and align the top raw edges. There should be a border of curtain fabric showing all around the lining. Pin the curtain and lining together along their top raw edges. Pin, baste and slip stitch the folded edges of the lining to the curtain. Leave the bottom of the lining open, as the curtain will hang better.

8 Cut the pencil pleat heading tape to the width of the curtain, plus an additional 3 cm (1¼ in) at each end. Knot the strings at the leading edge and leave them loose at the other.

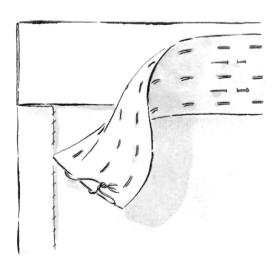

9 At the top raw edge of the curtain, turn down an 8 cm (3 in) fold to the wrong side. Press in place. Position the heading tape along the top of the curtain, 1 cm (½ in) below the folded top edge. Tuck under the raw ends of the tape and the knotted strings at the leading edge. The turnover will be concealed by the heading tape. Pin, baste and machine stitch around the edges of the heading tape through all the layers of fabric.

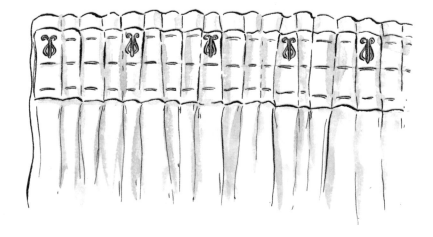

10 Pull the strings in the heading tape so that even gathers form across the front of the curtain. Knot the ends. Insert the curtain hooks into the tape at regular intervals, then hang the curtains from curtain rings or track.

headings

A curtain is attached to a track, rail or pole by the heading — the decorative top of the curtain. From formal pleated headings hung from antique poles with elaborate gilt finials, to informal ties loosely knotted round an iron rail, the heading sets the mood for the curtains. A wide variety of heading tapes is now available, so creating pinch pleats, goblet pleats, soft gathers and many other heading styles is now easier and more achievable than ever before.

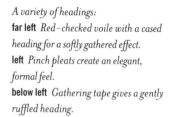

A variety of headings:
far left *Red-checked voile with a cased heading for a softly gathered effect.*
left *Pinch pleats create an elegant, formal feel.*
below left *Gathering tape gives a gently ruffled heading.*

below far left *A tightly gathered pencil pleat heading gives a ruched effect that adds interest to plain cream curtains.*
below centre *A simple heading with rings attached to hooks.*
below right *Unusual double curtains are attached to a pair of poles by means of clip-on curtain rings, which require no sewing.*

bottom *A crisp checked curtain with neatly knotted ties.*

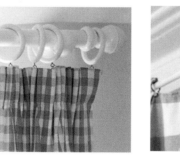

above and above left *Two examples of knotted ties. This is a simple and informal style of heading that works very well when curtains are not too weighty. Curtains with a tie heading must be drawn manually.*

left *A sunshiny yellow ticking with a tiny loop heading is strung across the bottom half of a window on string knotted to brass-headed nails.*

below left *Slotted onto a length of vivid braided red string, this checked curtain with a cased heading has a casual utilitarian feel.*

below *A simple cream curtain hanging from a classic wooden pole is enlivened by the addition of a chenille bobble fringe all along the loosely gathered heading.*

reversible scallops

These cosy quilted curtains could not be more simple to make. The fabric is reversible, so the curtains do not require a lining, and the scalloped top of the curtain simply flops over to act as a valance, showing the other side of the fabric. The curtains are attached to the pole with unobtrusive clip-on brass curtain rings, dispensing with the need for a sewn heading. The contrasting binding adds definition to the deeply scalloped edges of the valance.

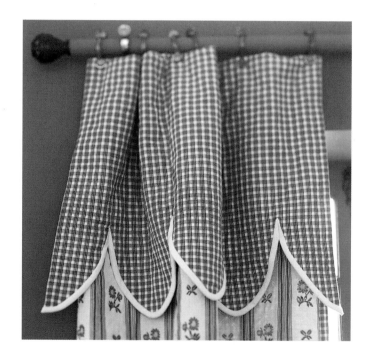

materials & equipment

reversible quilted fabric

bias binding

clip-on brass curtain rings

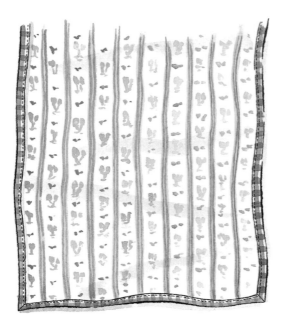

1 Measure your window to calculate fabric quantities (see Techniques, page 96). Unless it is very wide, you should only need one width of material for each curtain. Add an extra 60 cm (24 in) to the length for the overhang at the top, and 8 cm (3 in) for the hem.

2 Decide which side of the reversible fabric will be on the the front of the curtain and which will be on the back and valance. Press in a 1.5 cm (⅝ in), then a 2.5 cm (1 in) fold along the side and bottom edges to the front of the curtain. Mitre the corners and pin, baste and machine stitch in place. The hems act as a decorative border on the front of the curtain.

3 Make a template for the scalloped edge of the valance (see Templates, page 102). Make sure the width of the curtain is divisible by the width of the scallop to give an exact number of scallops across the curtain. Mark around the template on the wrong side of the fabric. There should be half a scallop at each side of the curtain. Remove the template and cut along the marked line.

4 Buy ready-made bias binding or make your own (see Techniques, page 101). You will need one continuous binding strip that is two and a half times the width of the curtain. Press in a 5 mm (¼ in) fold to the wrong side all along one long edge of the binding.

5 To bind the raw edges of the scallops, place the binding right side down on the back of the curtain, lining up the raw edges. Pin and baste the binding in place around all the scallops and half scallops, leaving 1 cm (½ in) extra binding at each side. Machine stitch the binding in place using a 1 cm (½ in) seam allowance.

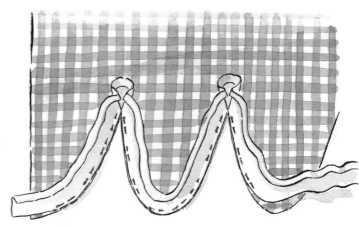

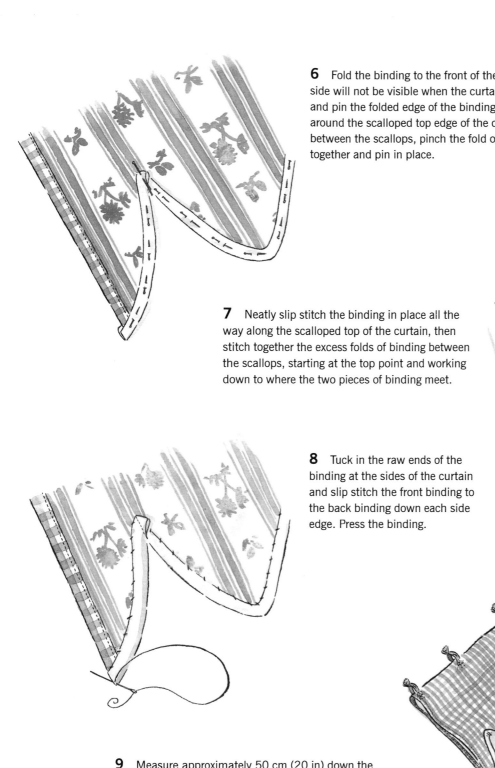

6 Fold the binding to the front of the curtain (this side will not be visible when the curtain is hanging) and pin the folded edge of the binding all the way around the scalloped top edge of the curtain. In between the scallops, pinch the fold of excess fabric together and pin in place.

7 Neatly slip stitch the binding in place all the way along the scalloped top of the curtain, then stitch together the excess folds of binding between the scallops, starting at the top point and working down to where the two pieces of binding meet.

8 Tuck in the raw ends of the binding at the sides of the curtain and slip stitch the front binding to the back binding down each side edge. Press the binding.

9 Measure approximately 50 cm (20 in) down the curtain from the scalloped edge and fold the curtain over to the right side at this point. The scalloped edge will fall on the front of the curtain and form a valance. Press along the fold line.

10 Position the clip-on curtain rings along the folded top of the curtain at approximately 20 cm (8 in) intervals. Hang the curtain from the curtain pole, ruffling it evenly. If the curtain is too long or too short for the window, adjust the depth of the valance fold accordingly.

button-on silk

A luxurious heavy swathe of raw silk hangs in a dramatic single sweep at a sash window, caught to one side by the squiggle of a minimalist metal hold-back. At the top of the curtain, tabs of the same fabric are buttoned on to the top of the curtain and hooked over small shell-shaped knobs. The fluid swags and folds of the fabric provide a classical flavour, but the unusual heading brings an unexpected modern twist to this simple arrangement.

materials & equipment

heavy raw silk

3 or 4 small, decorative drawer or cupboard knobs

6 to 8 silk-covered buttons

metal tieback

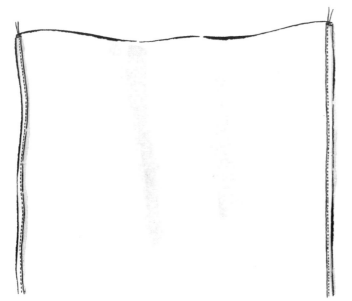

1 To calculate how much fabric is required, measure your window (see Techniques, page 96). The curtain must be the width of the window plus enough extra fabric to allow the curtain to swag between the knobs that it is buttoned to. Add an extra 27 cm (10¾ in) to the length for hem and heading and 12 cm (4¾ in) to the width for side hems. Join widths if necessary (see Techniques, page 98).

2 Press in a double 3 cm (1¼ in) hem to the wrong side down each side of the curtain, and pin, baste and machine stitch in place.

3 Press in a double 6 cm (2½ in) fold to the wrong side all the way across the top of the curtain. Pin, baste and machine stitch in place.

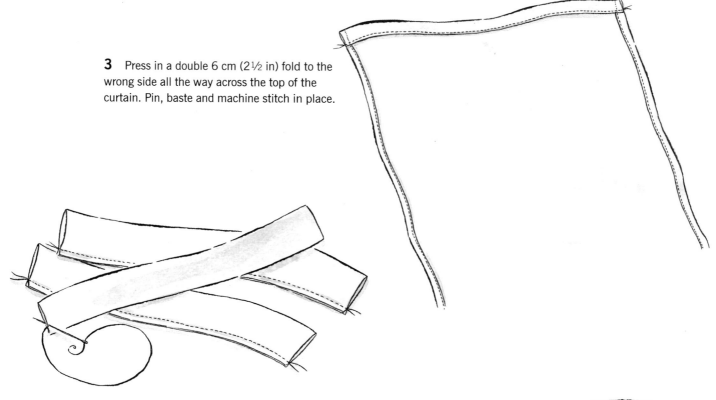

4 Decide how many knobs you are going to hang your curtain from (this will depend on the width of your window frame) and screw them to the wall or the top of the window frame at regular intervals. You will need one tab for each knob. Cut out a strip of silk 26 x 8 cm (10½ x 3 in) for each tab. Make up the tabs (see Techniques, page 101).

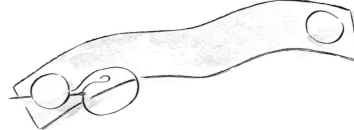

5 You will need two silk-covered buttons for each tab. Hand stitch a button 2.5 cm (1 in) in from each end of the tab.

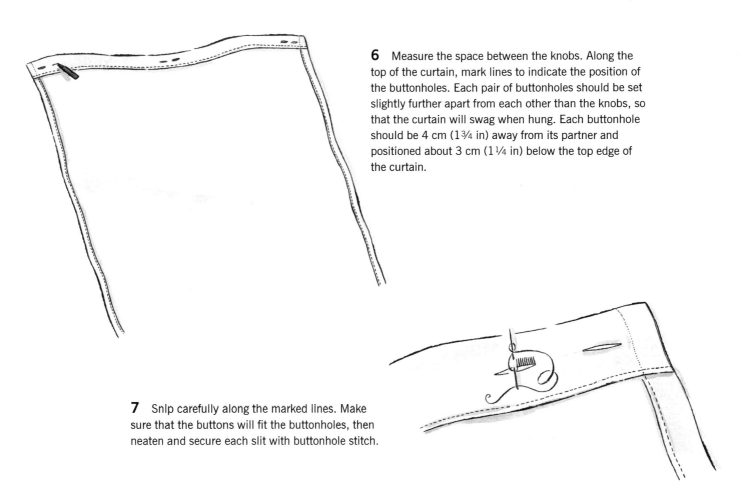

6 Measure the space between the knobs. Along the top of the curtain, mark lines to indicate the position of the buttonholes. Each pair of buttonholes should be set slightly further apart from each other than the knobs, so that the curtain will swag when hung. Each buttonhole should be 4 cm (1¾ in) away from its partner and positioned about 3 cm (1¼ in) below the top edge of the curtain.

7 Snip carefully along the marked lines. Make sure that the buttons will fit the buttonholes, then neaten and secure each slit with buttonhole stitch.

8 Button each tab to the curtain, then hook the loops over the knobs to hang the curtain. Measure a hem line with pins and take the curtain down again. Fold up a double hem at the bottom of the curtain and pin, baste and machine stitch in place.

9 Press and rehang the curtain. Attach a metal holdback at one side of the window. This will allow you to loop the curtain to one side of the window.

concertina stripes

Heavy striped cloth curtains hang in neat, regimented folds that accentuate the height of the window and create a smart tailored effect. These curtains are stiffened with interfacing, which ensures that the crisp concertina folds hold their shape perfectly. The simplicity of the arrangement is complemented by the ingenious use of eyelets and tension wire to hang the curtains, dispensing with the need for a conventional heading.

materials & equipment

striped cotton fabric

iron-on or sew-in interfacing

fabric glue

2.5 cm (1 in) diameter metal eyelets

hole punch kit

tension wire to fit across window

1   To calculate fabric quantities, measure the window (see Techniques, page 96). Each finished curtain must be the width of the window plus 6 cm (2½ in) for side hems. Add 20 cm (8 in) to the length for hem and heading.

2   Cut out the curtain fabric. Join widths if necessary (see Techniques, page 98). Cut enough interfacing for the reverse of the curtain. To join widths of interfacing, butt the pieces up to each other rather than overlapping them. Place the main fabric right side down, and lay the interfacing on top. Pin and baste the interfacing to the main curtain all around the edges.

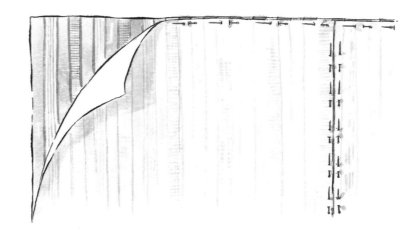

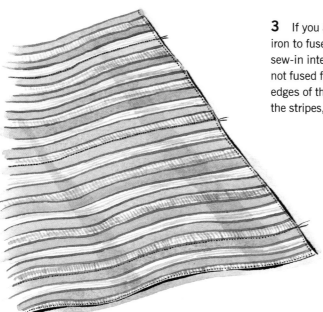

3   If you are using iron-on interfacing, use a warm iron to fuse it to the back of the main fabric. For sew-in interfacing, or if your iron-on interfacing has not fused fully, machine stitch around the outer edges of the curtain and, following the verticals of the stripes, run a few parallel seams down the length.

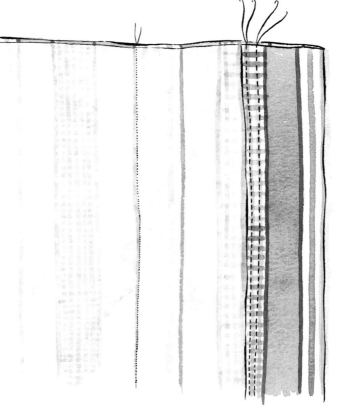

4   Turn in a 3 cm (1¼ in) hem to the wrong side down both sides of the curtain. Press. Pin and baste the hems. Machine stitch two parallel lines of stitching down each side of the curtain to hold the hems in place.

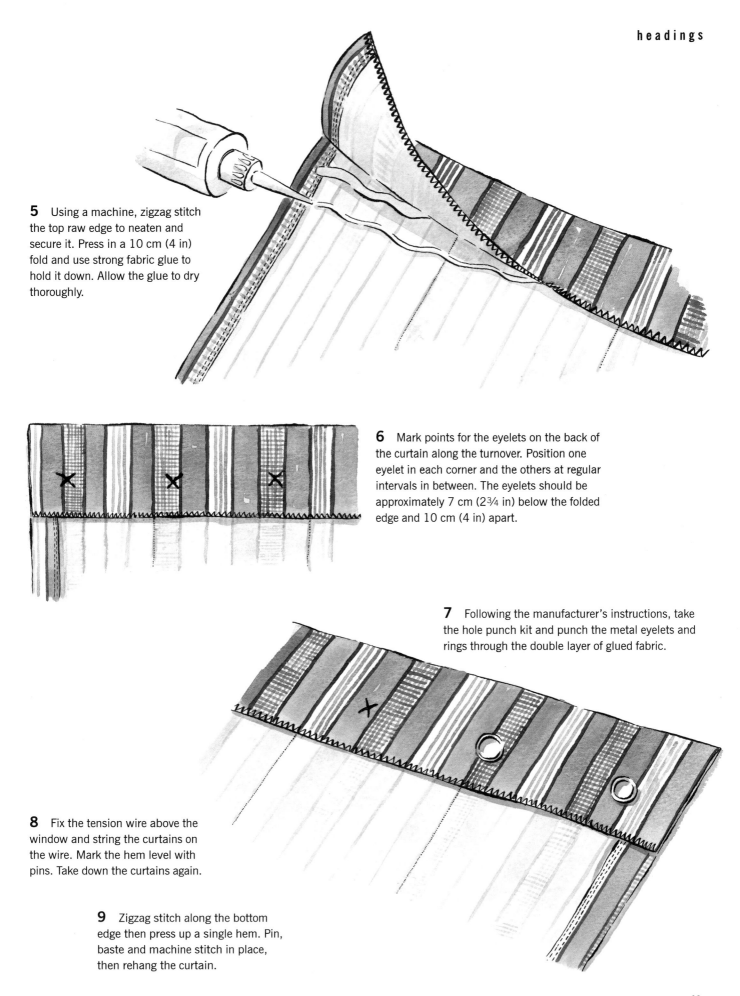

5 Using a machine, zigzag stitch the top raw edge to neaten and secure it. Press in a 10 cm (4 in) fold and use strong fabric glue to hold it down. Allow the glue to dry thoroughly.

6 Mark points for the eyelets on the back of the curtain along the turnover. Position one eyelet in each corner and the others at regular intervals in between. The eyelets should be approximately 7 cm (2¾ in) below the folded edge and 10 cm (4 in) apart.

7 Following the manufacturer's instructions, take the hole punch kit and punch the metal eyelets and rings through the double layer of glued fabric.

8 Fix the tension wire above the window and string the curtains on the wire. Mark the hem level with pins. Take down the curtains again.

9 Zigzag stitch along the bottom edge then press up a single hem. Pin, baste and machine stitch in place, then rehang the curtain.

tie-on muslin sheers

These floaty unlined muslin curtains hanging at a French window create a light and airy atmosphere. The wrought-iron pole is attached not to the window frame but to the ceiling, and the length of the curtains and the swathes of fabric emphasize rather than obscure the fine proportions of the elegant glass doors. The bobbly tassel fringe provides a textural contrast with the economical outlines of the simple metal tie-back.

materials & equipment

white muslin

tassel fringing

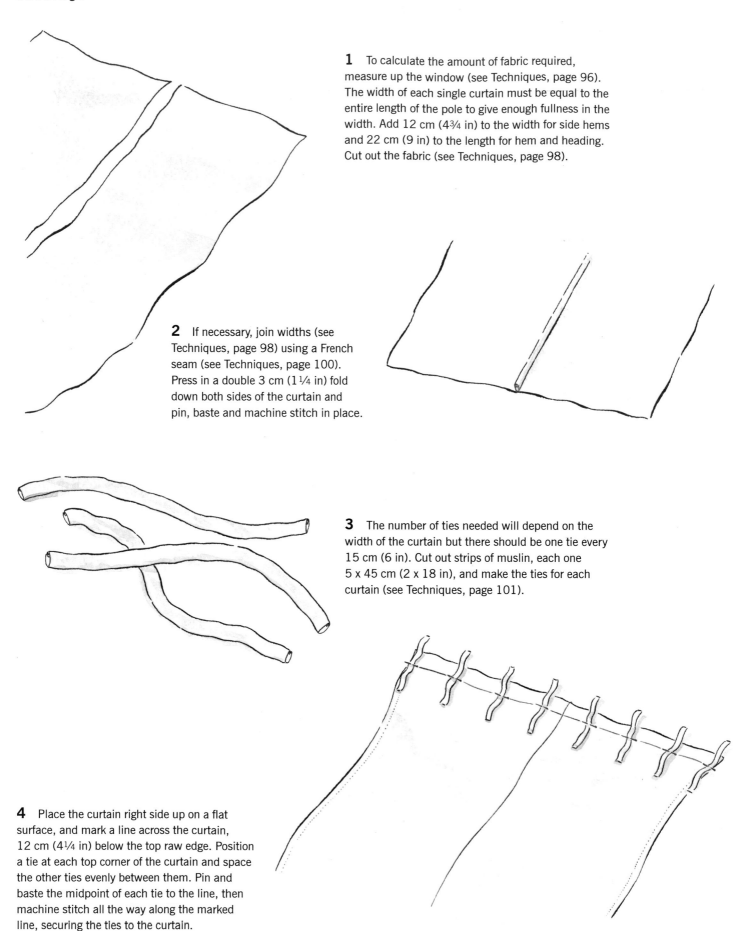

1   To calculate the amount of fabric required, measure up the window (see Techniques, page 96). The width of each single curtain must be equal to the entire length of the pole to give enough fullness in the width. Add 12 cm (4¾ in) to the width for side hems and 22 cm (9 in) to the length for hem and heading. Cut out the fabric (see Techniques, page 98).

2   If necessary, join widths (see Techniques, page 98) using a French seam (see Techniques, page 100). Press in a double 3 cm (1¼ in) fold down both sides of the curtain and pin, baste and machine stitch in place.

3   The number of ties needed will depend on the width of the curtain but there should be one tie every 15 cm (6 in). Cut out strips of muslin, each one 5 x 45 cm (2 x 18 in), and make the ties for each curtain (see Techniques, page 101).

4   Place the curtain right side up on a flat surface, and mark a line across the curtain, 12 cm (4¼ in) below the top raw edge. Position a tie at each top corner of the curtain and space the other ties evenly between them. Pin and baste the midpoint of each tie to the line, then machine stitch all the way along the marked line, securing the ties to the curtain.

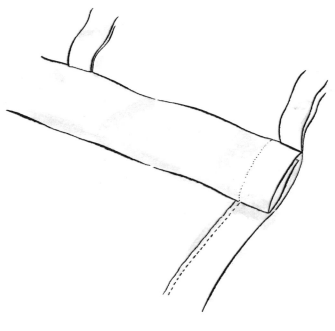

5 Turn the curtain over so it is wrong side up. Make a fold along the line of stitching just made at the top of the curtain. Press the fold in place. Then turn in the folded edge again to make a double 6 cm (2½ in) fold.

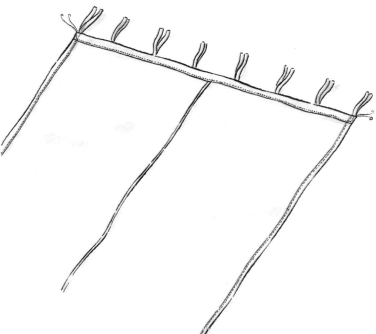

6 Pin, baste and machine stitch the fold in place, stitching all around the long edges and short sides.

7 Hang the curtain by knotting the ties to the pole. Measure the hem level and mark with pins. Take the curtain down again and fold up a double hem. Pin, baste and machine sew the hem in place.

8 To trim the curtain, pin a continuous length of tassel fringe to the wrong side of the curtain, all the way down the leading edge and across the bottom. Slip stitch the trimming in place. Press and rehang the curtains.

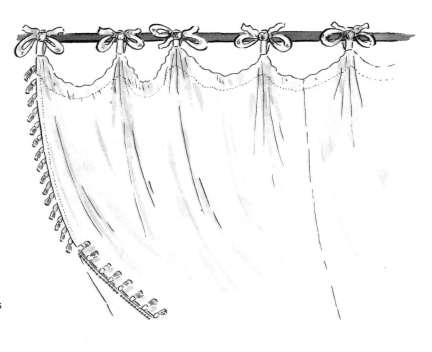

valances and pelmets

Pelmets and valances add a perfect finishing touch to an attractive window treatment. Pelmets are stiffened, shaped pieces of fabric attached to a pelmet board. Valances are softer in effect and gathered, and are suspended from a pole, track or pelmet board. Both can be used alone or teamed with matching or contrasting curtains.

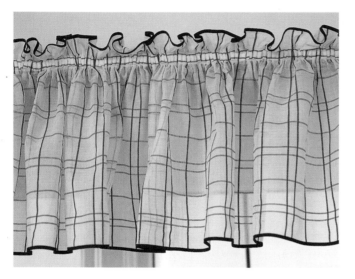

left *A checked voile valance is edged top and bottom with a thin red trim, which emphasizes the tight ruffles of the gathering tape heading. Valances are ideally suited to windows that do not need a full curtain.*

below left *This panel of fabric acts as a valance at a small kitchen window. Small-scale red-and-white gingham has a cased heading into which an expansion rod has been inserted. The fabric is held out of the way with thin ties. A quick and easy window treatment that need not be a permanent fixture.*

below right *An unassuming pair of striped cotton curtains is made much more imposing by the addition of a classic-shaped pelmet. Vertically striped curtains and pelmets can appear to lengthen the proportions of small, wide windows.*

above *A bold Gothic-inspired pelmet covered in a rich red linen. This type of pelmet uses buckram, a stiffened hessian fabric, which can hold the desired shape. Shaped and stiffened pelmets such as this one are guaranteed to add an air of importance to a window treatment and are especially useful for screening an unsightly window top.*

above centre *This cheerful checked curtain is self-valanced — the valance is a separate piece of the same fabric sewn to the top of the curtain. Heading tape has been attached to the back of the curtain just below the join. A contrasting border defines the leading edge of the curtains and the bottom of the valance.*

above right *A more traditional and formal pelmet treatment. A wooden pelmet board has been covered tightly with fabric that matches the curtains, then attached to the wall just above the curtain track with a pair of brackets. The box-pleated skirt has been either stapled or Velcroed to the pelmet board. The pelmet is trimmed with narrow binding in a complementary colour.*

right *In a small bathroom, the window is screened by a sheer fabric panel and deep pelmet, which do not block the light as conventional curtains do. The bold pelmet, with its scalloped edges, is made from large-scale gingham checks and edged with small-scale gingham, cut on the bias.*

gathered gingham

With its crisp checks and primary colours, gingham has a fresh, countrified charm and is ideally suited to kitchens and bathrooms. Here, it has been used to create an informal window treatment that could not be simpler to make. Unlined curtains with a cased heading are slotted on to a metal rod or curtain wire. Cased headings cannot be drawn open or closed, so to conceal the rod a separate valance has been made to hang in between the curtains.

materials & equipment

cotton gingham fabric
extending metal rod or curtain wire

1 Measure up your window to calculate fabric quantities (see Techniques, page 96). The valance should be approximately a quarter of the length of the curtains. Add 25 cm (10 in) to the length of the curtains and valance for hems and headings.

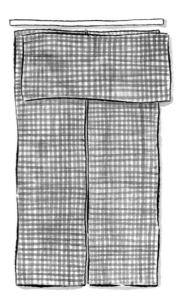

2 Each curtain occupies a quarter of the width of the window, while the valance occupies half of the width. The combined width of the finished, ungathered curtains and valance should be at least twice the width of your rod or wire. Add 4 cm (1¾ in) to the width for side hems.

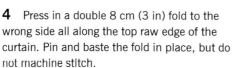

3 Cut out both the curtains and the valance. If necessary, join widths (see Techniques, page 98) using a French seam (see Techniques, page 100). Place one curtain on a flat surface, right side down. Press in a double 1 cm (½ in) hem down each side of the curtain. Pin, baste and machine sew in place. Repeat for the valance and other curtain.

4 Press in a double 8 cm (3 in) fold to the wrong side all along the top raw edge of the curtain. Pin and baste the fold in place, but do not machine stitch.

5 Using a fabric pen, mark two parallel lines all along the fold at the top of the curtain. The first line should be 4 cm (1¾ in) below the top folded edge of the curtain, and the second line 2 cm (¾ in) below that. Machine sew down the marked lines, always stitching in the same direction to prevent the fabric from puckering. Repeat steps 3 and 4 on the valance and other curtain.

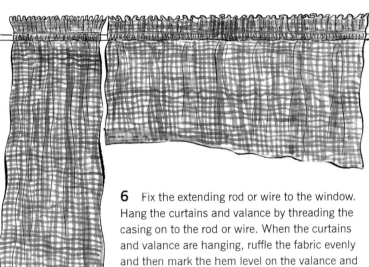

6 Fix the extending rod or wire to the window. Hang the curtains and valance by threading the casing on to the rod or wire. When the curtains and valance are hanging, ruffle the fabric evenly and then mark the hem level on the valance and curtains with pins.

7 Remove the curtains and valance from the rod, and along the bottom edges turn up double hems, mitring the corners. Press the hems then pin, baste and machine stitch in place. Slip stitch the mitres.

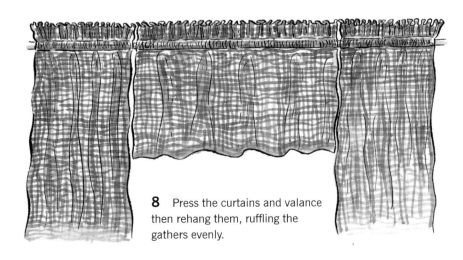

8 Press the curtains and valance then rehang them, ruffling the gathers evenly.

monogrammed linen valance

This linen valance has been decorated with a machine-embroidered initial, but its fluid folds and majestic proportions would be just as effective if it were plain. The valance is designed to hang alone, but can be combined with unlined curtains in the same fabric, suspended from eyelets screwed into the bottom of the pelmet board.

materials & equipment

heavy linen fabric

lining fabric

staple gun

2 cm (³/₄ in) thick plywood for the pelmet board

angle brackets

1 Make the pelmet board (see Techniques, page 98). To calculate fabric quantities, measure the board (see Techniques, page 97). Add 72 cm (29 in) to the width for the pleats at the sides of the valance. The centre of the valance should measure a third of the drop from pelmet board to floor.

2 A strip of main fabric is needed to act as a hem on the back of the valance. Add 30 cm (12 in) to the length of the valance for this hem strip. The lining fabric must be 30 cm (12 in) shorter than the main fabric as it does not include additional fabric for a hem strip. Cut out the fabric for the valance and lining. If you want to embroider or otherwise decorate the central panel, do so at this point, before joining widths.

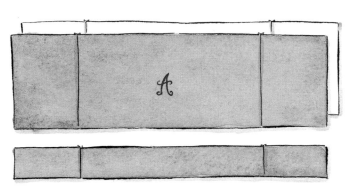

3 Join widths (see Techniques, page 98). Place a width in the centre of the valance with part widths on either side. Measure 30 cm (12 in) up from the bottom edge of the valance and mark a line across the width of the valance. Cut along the line. This strip of main fabric will be the hem strip. The valance should now be the same size as the lining.

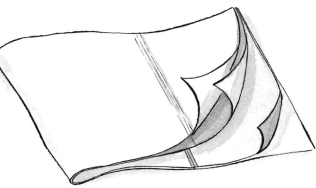

4 Make a template for the bottom edge of the valance (see Templates, page 104). Pin the lining and fabric together, right sides facing. Fold in half widthways, linen fabric right sides together, so the lining is uppermost.

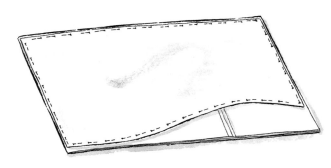

5 Pin the template to the lining and mark around it. Remove the template and cut along the marked line. Open out the valance.

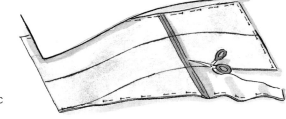

6 Fold the hem strip in half widthways, right sides together. Pin the template to the folded strip, so the lowest point of the template rests on the bottom edge of the fabric, and mark around it. Unpin the template, move it up 12 cm (4¾ in) and pin to the fabric again. Mark a second line, parallel to the first. Cut along both lines to create a shaped hem strip that matches the bottom of the valance.

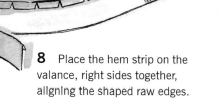

7 Press in a 1.5 cm (⅝ in) fold to the wrong side along the top edge of the hem strip. Clip the curves so the fabric lies flat.

8 Place the hem strip on the valance, right sides together, aligning the shaped raw edges.

9 Place the lining on the valance, right side down, the strip sandwiched in between the two. Make sure all raw edges are exactly aligned. Pin, baste and machine stitch along the raw shaped edges using a 1.5 cm (⅝ in) seam allowance. Clip the seam.

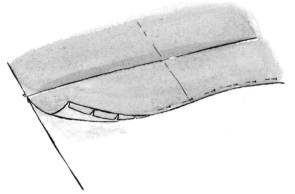

10 Open the valance out. Pin, baste and machine stitch the folded top edge of the hem strip to the right side of the lining.

11 Press in a 1.5 cm (⅝ in) hem along the raw side edges of the valance and lining. Neatly slip stitch the folded edges of the lining and valance together.

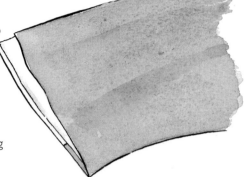

12 Along the top of the valance, zigzag stitch the edges of the lining and main fabric together, to neaten and secure the raw edges.

13 Mark a line around the top of the board, 5 cm (2 in) from the edge. Align the centre of the valance with the centre of the board. Using a staple gun, staple the fabric to the board, lining up the zigzagged edges with the marked line. Approximately 12 cm (4¾ in) away from each short end, fold a 10 cm (4 in) box pleat and staple in place (see Techniques, page 101).

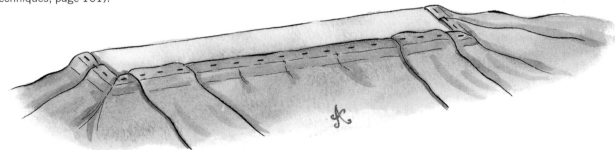

14 Work the fabric round the corner of the board and fold two 4 cm (1¾ in) knife pleats at the short end, stapling them in place. Repeat at the other end. Fix the brackets to the board, position it above the window and hang the pelmet board and valance.

beaded zigzags

The bold outlines of this colourful zigzagged valance draw attention to an attractive bay window without obscuring the view or the light. The valance, with its simple shape and rich colours, has an artless, naive charm, emphasized by the wooden beads that dangle from the zigzags. The vertical stripes have been turned to the horizontal in the contrasting heading strip. Gingham half-curtains screen the lower part of the window.

materials & equipment

striped cotton fabric

lining fabric

piping cord

2.5 cm (1 in) deep gathering tape

decorative hanging beads

curtain hooks

1 To calculate how much material is needed, measure your window (see Techniques, page 96).

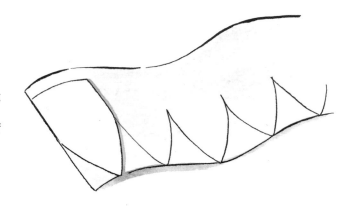

2 The valance is gathered at the top using gathering tape, which requires fabric two and a half times the width of the pole. The valance should occupy a fifth of the drop from pole to floor. Add 1.5 cm (⅝ in) seam allowance all round. The lining must be 15 cm (6 in) deeper than the main fabric. Cut out the valance and lining fabrics.

3 Make a zigzag template (see Templates, page 102). The width of the valance fabric must be divisible by the width of the zigzag to give an exact number of zigzags across the valance. Mark around the template on the wrong side of the fabric. Repeat with the lining, but leave an additional 15 cm (6 in) of fabric at the top edge. Cut along the marked outline.

4 For the contrasting heading, join pieces of fabric to make a strip of horizontally striped fabric that is the width of the finished valance and 16 cm (6½ in) deep. Lay the front panel of the valance on a flat surface, right side up. Place the strip on top of it, right side down, top straight edges aligning. Pin, baste and machine stitch 1.5 cm (⅝ in) from the raw edge.

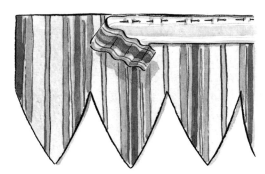

5 Make a length of piping (see Techniques, page 101) that is two and a half times the width of the valance.

6 Place the lining on a flat surface, right side up, and, lining up the raw edges, pin and baste the piping all around the zigzagged bottom edge of the lining.

7 Place the front panel right side down on top of the lining. Pin and baste the layers together, taking in the piping. Using a piping foot, machine stitch all around the sides and the zigzagged bottom of the valance, making sure that the piping cord is inside the stitching.

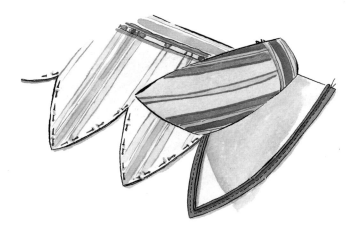

8 Clip around the zigzags, so that when you turn the valance right side out the zigzags will lie flat and will not pucker.

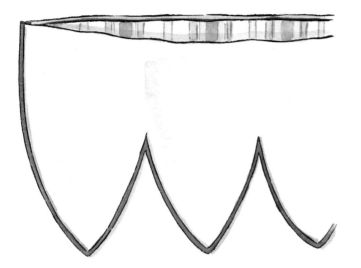

9 Turn the valance right side out. Poke out the points of the zigzags with a knitting needle. Press a 1.5 cm (⅝ in) fold to the inside all the way along both the open straight edges at the top of the valance.

10 Cut the heading tape to the width of the valance. Knot the threads at one end but leave them loose at the other. Pin and baste the heading tape along the top edge of the back of the valance, making sure that the top edge of the heading tape aligns with the folded top edges of the valance and tucking the raw ends of the tape under at both ends. Machine stitch all around the heading tape, close to the edges.

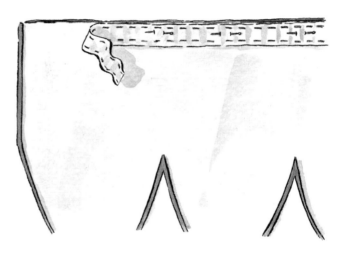

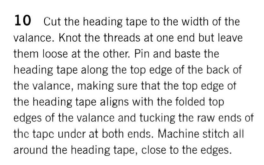

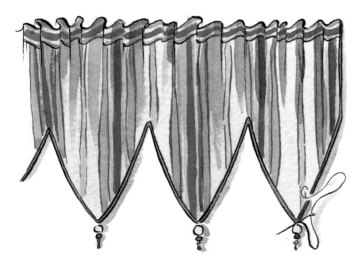

11 Pull the strings of the tape into a loose gather, and knot the end. Hand sew two or three beads to the very tip of each zigzag for decoration.

12 Insert the curtain hooks at even intervals along the tape. Hang the valance from curtain rings on your pole.

red-trimmed voile

This simple yet stylish all-in-one single curtain and valance is ideally suited to French windows. The semi-translucent voile allows sunlight to filter into the room, creating a warm glow of diffused light. The voluminous folds of the voile feel wonderfully lavish, while the vivid scarlet ribbon adds definition to the valance. If the door is frequently in use, a metal hold-back fixed to the side of it would allow the curtain to be neatly caught to one side, out of the way.

materials & equipment

white voile fabric

3 cm (1 1/4 in) wide red silk bindings

clip-on curtain rings

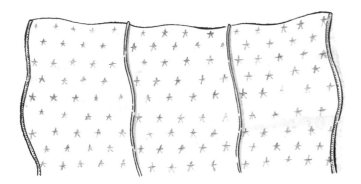

1   Measure the window to calculate fabric quantities (see Techniques, page 96). Add 7 cm (2¾ in) to the length for the hem. The fabric must be three times the width of the pole plus 12 cm (4¾ in) for side hems. Cut out the fabric. Join widths using a French seam (see Techniques, page 100). Pin, baste and machine stitch a double 3 cm (1¼ in) hem down each side of the curtain.

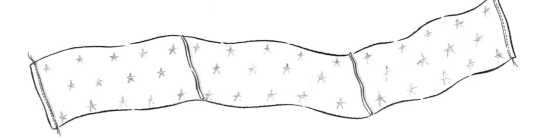

2   The valance should be one sixth of the length of the finished curtain and the same width plus hem allowances. Cut out the fabric then join widths as for the main curtain. Press in a double 3 cm (1¼ in) hem down each side. Pin, baste and machine stitch in place.

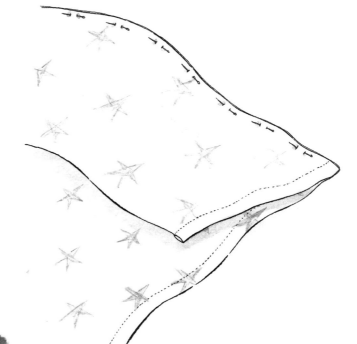

3   Place the valance right side up on top of the right side of the main curtain, lining up the raw edges at the top. Pin, baste and machine stitch together using a 1 cm (½ in) seam allowance.

4   Make two strips of red silk binding (see Techniques, page 101). Each strip should be equal to the width of the curtain plus 2.5 cm (1 in) for the end turnings. Turn in and press 5 mm (¼ in) to the wrong side along the long edges of the binding. Then press the strips in half so that the folded edges meet.

5 Insert the top seamed edges of the curtain and valance into the folded binding. Pin and baste the binding in place along the front and back of the curtain.

6 Zigzag machine stitch the binding in place, stitching on the front of the curtain along the folded edge of the binding. Use thread that is the same colour as the binding. Tuck in the raw ends of the binding and close with a few neat stitches.

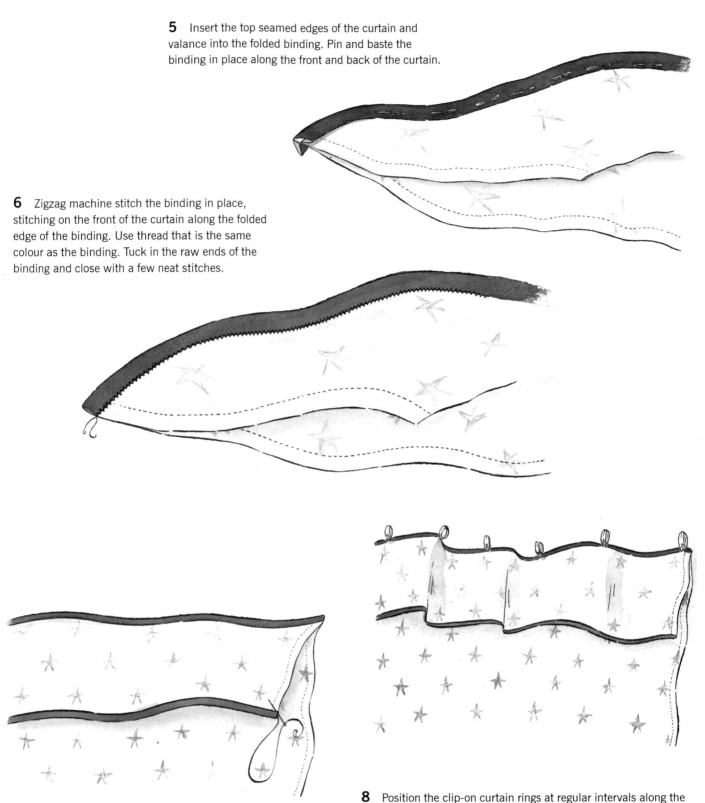

7 Insert the bottom edge of the valance into the second strip of binding. Pin, baste and machine zigzag the binding in place, again using matching thread and tucking in the raw ends.

8 Position the clip-on curtain rings at regular intervals along the red binding at the top of the curtain. Thread the curtain on to the pole. Once the curtain is hanging, measure the hem level and mark it with pins. Take the curtain off the pole, and along the bottom edge fold under a double hem. Pin, baste and machine stitch the hem in place. Finally, slip stitch closed the open sides of the hem. Press and rehang the curtain.

shaped linen valance

This softly flowing linen valance adds interest to the simple proportions of a shuttered balcony window and provides a focal point in an understated interior. An unusual contrasting border emphasizes the gentle gathers of the shaped bottom edge. The valance has a simple yet effective cased heading that can be simply slotted on to a curtain pole or rod, while unobtrusive finials hold the soft gathers of the valance in place.

materials & equipment

linen or thick cotton fabric
contrasting linen or thick cotton fabric for the border

1 Measure the window to calculate fabric quantities (see Techniques, page 96). The valance is slightly gathered so must be half as wide again as the pole. The deepest part of the valance occupies a quarter of the drop from pole to floor. It is self-lined, so double the amount of fabric needed and add 3 cm (1¼ in) all round for hems and seams.

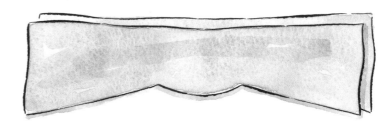

2 You will also need contrasting fabric for the border. The border strip, when joined, should be the width of the valance and 11 cm (4½ in) deep. Make templates for the border pieces (see Templates, page 103). Place the templates on the contrasting fabric, mark around them, then cut out the border.

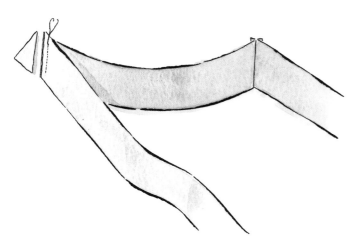

3 Join the border pieces. Line up one short end of the crescent-shaped strip with the short end of a side strip, right sides facing, and pin and baste together at a 45 degree angle. Check that the angle of the seam is correct, then machine stitch the seam. Join the other end of the crescent to the other strip in the same way. Trim the seams.

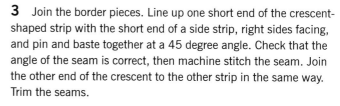

4 Turn in and press a 1.5 cm (⅝ in) fold all around the raw edges of the border on the wrong side. Clip the curved edges so the fabric lies flat.

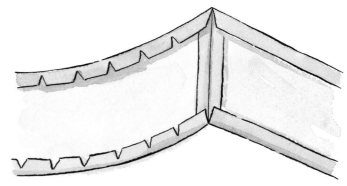

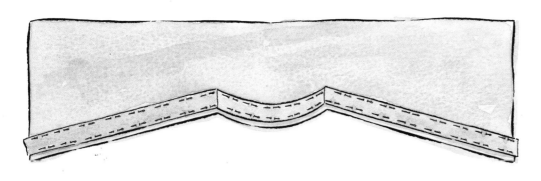

5 Cut out the front and back of the valance, using the border template as a guide for the shaped edge. Pin the border strip to the front panel, right side up, 2.5 cm (1 in) above the raw edge. Baste and machine stitch in place.

6   Place the front and back panels right sides together, aligning all edges. Pin, baste and machine stitch along the straight top edge using a 1.5 cm (⅝ in) seam allowance. Open out the valance and press the seam open.

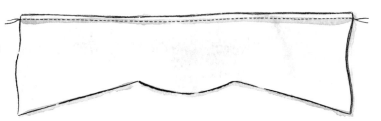

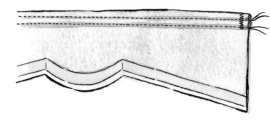

7   Press a 5 mm (¼ in) fold to the wrong side along the side edges of the valance, then press in a second 1 cm (½ in) fold. Pin, baste and slip stitch the side hem in place. To reinforce the valance, zigzag stitch a 16 cm (6½ in) seam across the central seam, 2.5 cm (1 in) in from the side edges.

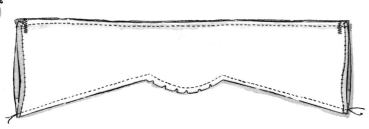

8   Fold the valance so the front and back panels are right sides together. Pin, baste and machine stitch along the raw bottom edge, using a 1.5 cm (⅝ in) seam allowance. Clip the curves so the fabric lies flat.

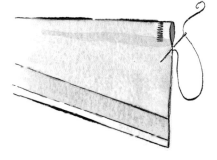

9   Turn the valance right side out. Slip stitch the folded side edges of the valance together, working from the bottom up to the zigzag stitching, 8 cm (3 in) from the top of the valance.

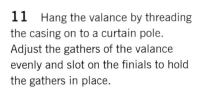

10   Using a fabric pen, mark two parallel lines across the full width of the valance, the first line 4 cm (1¾ in) below the top edge and the second 4 cm (1¾ in) beneath the first. Machine stitch along the two lines to create a casing that can be then be threaded over the curtain pole to hang the valance.

11   Hang the valance by threading the casing on to a curtain pole. Adjust the gathers of the valance evenly and slot on the finials to hold the gathers in place.

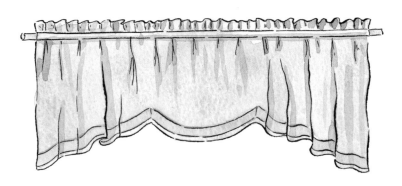

rope-edged valance

The jolly stripes, wavy bottom, and coordinating rope trim of this slightly gathered valance give it a cheerful nautical air. It is an ideal summer replacement for heavy full-length curtains, which are perfect for the winter months but can appear oppressive and cumbersome during warmer weather. The valance allows plenty of summer sunlight to flood into the room, yet prevents the window from looking too bare and unfurnished.

materials & equipment

striped cotton fabric

thick rope trim

1   To calculate fabric quantities, measure the window (see Techniques, page 96). The length of the pole will dictate the finished width of the valance. The valance should hang down over about a fifth of the window. Add an extra 1.5 cm (⅝ in) seam allowance all round. Cut out two pieces of fabric, one for the front and one for the back of the valance. Remember that the stripes should run vertically.

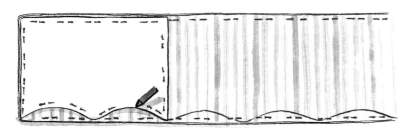

2   Make a template for the bottom edge of the valance (see Templates, page 104). Pin the front and back panels of fabric right sides together, then pin the template to the back panel. Draw around the template.

3   With the two panels still pinned together, cut along the marked line through both layers of fabric.

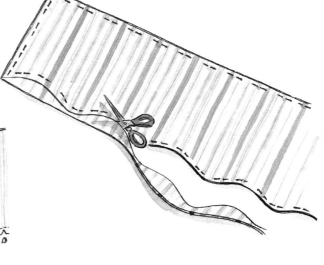

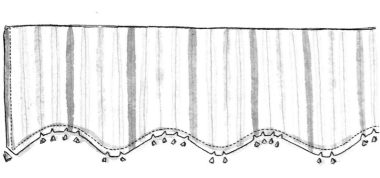

4   Baste and machine stitch along the sides and wavy bottom edge of the panel, using a 1.5 cm (⅝ in) seam allowance. Leave the top straight edge open. Trim the seam allowance and clip the curves and corners of the wavy edge to reduce any puckering or bulkiness.

5   The number of ties you need will depend on the width of the valance, but you should have a tie above every 'wave' along the bottom of the valance and one at each corner. Make the ties (see Techniques, page 101) and knot the ends of each tie.

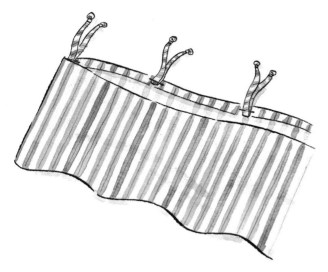

6 Turn the valance right side out. All along the top edges press in a 1.5 cm (⅝ in) fold to the inside of the valance. Fold each tie in half widthways and tuck them in between the top folded edges, positioning a tie at each end of the valance and spacing them at regular intervals in between.

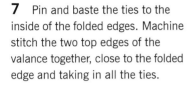

7 Pin and baste the ties to the inside of the folded edges. Machine stitch the two top edges of the valance together, close to the folded edge and taking in all the ties.

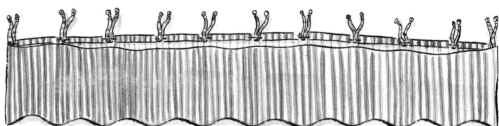

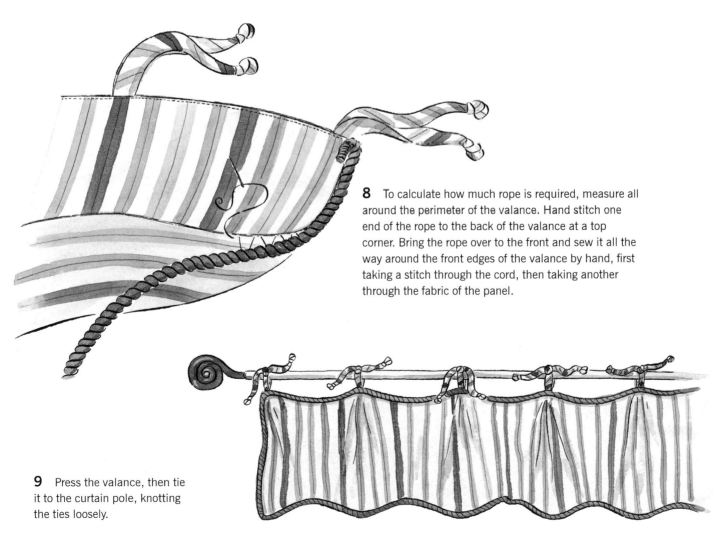

8 To calculate how much rope is required, measure all around the perimeter of the valance. Hand stitch one end of the rope to the back of the valance at a top corner. Bring the rope over to the front and sew it all the way around the front edges of the valance by hand, first taking a stitch through the cord, then taking another through the fabric of the panel.

9 Press the valance, then tie it to the curtain pole, knotting the ties loosely.

gypsy-skirted valance

This deeply ruffled valance is enriched by the addition of a printed border with an old-fashioned Middle European flavour. The naive charm of the valance is enhanced by the carved wooden beads that dangle from the lower edge. Other fabrics could be substituted for this bold Bohemian design — try a colourful paisley or Provençal print.

materials & equipment

heavy cotton fabric

border fabric

interlining

lining fabric

5 cm (2 in) deep pencil pleat heading tape

curtain hooks

decorative wooden beads

2 cm (³/₄ in) thick plywood for the pelmet board

angle brackets

metal eyelets

1 The valance hangs from a pelmet board. Calculate the size and position of the pelmet board and make the board (see Techniques, page 98). Screw eyelets around the edges at regular intervals. Attach the pelmet board to the wall.

2 Measure the pelmet board and window to calculate fabric quantities (see Techniques, page 96). The pencil pleat heading requires fabric two and a half times the width of the pelmet board. Add 8 cm (3 in) for side hems. The pelmet occupies one sixth of the drop from board to floor. Add 13 cm (5 in) for hem and heading. The border is two-thirds as deep as the main fabric and the same width. Add 3 cm (1¼ in) to the length and 8 cm (3 in) to the width for hems.

3 The lining and interlining should measure the same as the valance but without any additions for hems and seams. Cut out the fabric for the valance, border, lining and interlining, joining widths as necessary (see Techniques, page 98).

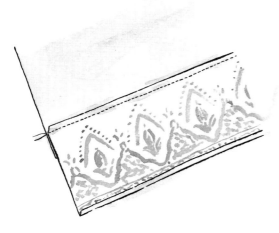

4 Press a 1.5 cm (⅝ in) fold over to the wrong side along the top edge of the border strip. Place the main material on a flat surface, right side up. Place the border right side down on top of the valance, the bottom raw edge overlapping with the bottom raw edge of the valance by 8 cm (3 in). Pin, baste and machine stitch the valance and border together along the raw bottom edge of the border, using a 1.5 cm (⅝ in) seam allowance.

5 Fold the border up so it is lying on the front of the valance. Pin, baste and machine stitch along the top folded edge of the border, so it is firmly attached to the main material.

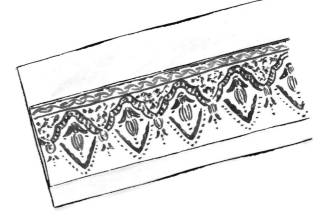

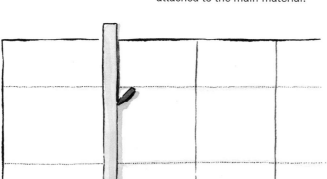

6 Place the valance right side down on a flat surface. Using fabric pen and a ruler, draw vertical lines every 30 cm (12 in) all the way across the back of the valance.

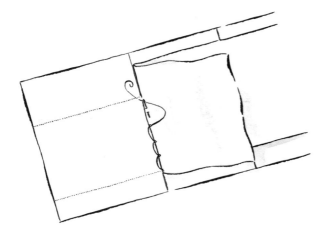

7 Place the interlining on top of the valance, 5 cm (2 in) below the top raw edge, 8 cm (3 in) above the bottom raw edge and 4 cm (1¾ in) from each side. Fold back one side of the interlining to the first line. Working from bottom to top, lock stitch the interlining to the valance (see Techniques, page 99). Continue until the interlining is locked in across the entire width of the valance.

8 Press in a 4 cm (1¾ in) hem at each side of the valance and an 8 cm (3 in) hem along the bottom. Press in the angled mitres (see Techniques, page 100). Pin and baste the hems in place. Herringbone stitch the side and base hems and slip stitch the mitres.

9 Take the lining and press in a 2 cm (¾ in) fold along the short sides and a double 2 cm (¾ in) hem along the bottom. Mitre the corners (see Techniques, page 100). Pin, baste and machine stitch the side and bottom hems in place.

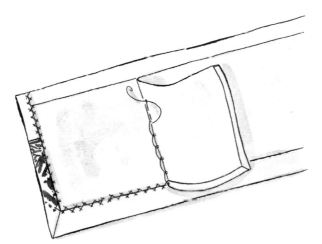

10 Place the lining on the valance, wrong sides together, the top raw edge of the lining 5 cm (2 in) below the top edge of the valance. As the valance is so wide, the lining must also be locked in across the width of the valance. Working across the valance, lock in the lining fabric as you locked in the interlining in steps 6 and 7.

11 When the lining is attached across the width of the valance, slip stitch the hemmed edges to the side hem of the valance. Leave the bottom of the lining loose, as the valance will hang better.

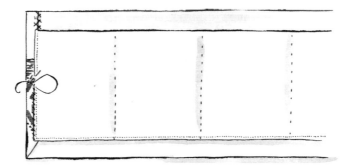

12 If desired, hand sew colourful wooden beads along the bottom edge of the valance at 5 cm (2 in) intervals.

13 Cut the heading tape to the width of the valance, plus an additional 3 cm (1¼ in) at each end. Knot the strings at one end of the tape and leave them loose at the other. At the top of the valance, turn a 5 cm (2 in) fold to the wrong side. Pin the heading tape over the fold, 1 cm (½ in) from the top edge, tucking under the raw ends of the tape. Baste and machine stitch all around the heading tape.

14 Pull the strings of the heading tape to gather the valance, then knot the ends. Insert as many curtain hooks as there are eyelets on the pelmet board, and hang the valance.

edgings

Adding an edging or border to a curtain will create an additional decorative element and subtly enliven even the most understated window treatment. From subtle scallops to tasselled trimming, edgings should be chosen to complement yet contrast with your curtain. And always remember that bold and simple edgings are more effective than fuss and flounce.

below left top and bottom *Shaggy silk fringing attached to the leading edge brings an intriguing tactile quality to a plain pair of curtains.*
below centre *A translucent voile panel edged with a wide grosgrain ribbon screens the view yet does not obscure the elegant lines of this window and full-length shutters.*
below *The backs of curtains are rarely as attractive as the fronts, but, these are decorative on both sides. The front of the curtain is a cheerful blue gingham while the back has a bold border.*

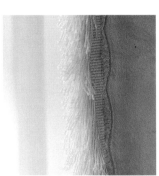

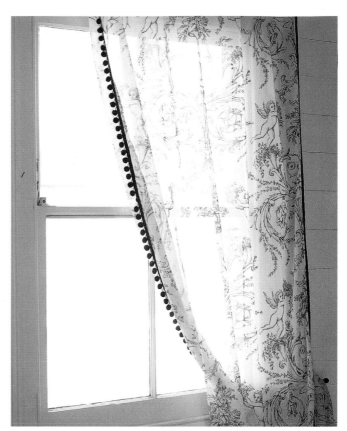

left, right and above *When used as an edging, bobble fringing adds an interesting textural element to any soft furnishings and will instantly transform even the dullest pair of curtains. It is available in a wide variety of colours and weights, making it a suitable trimming for almost every fabric. Attached to the leading edge of a curtain, it will add definition and interest.*

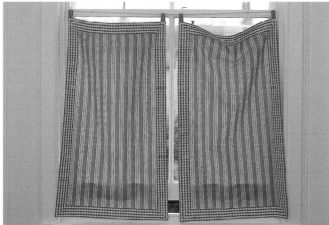

above *These two striped panels screening the bottom half of a sash window are edged with a wide border cut from a contrasting check in the same colour.*

right *A simple pair of floaty voile curtains is given an opulent, elegant feel with the addition of a fluffy tasselled fringe.*

far right *A printed border sewn to the bottom of plain cotton curtains imitates the effect of hand-stitched embroidery.*

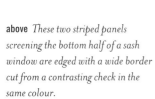

italian stringing with bow

These elegant blue-and-white checked curtains have a permanently fixed heading and are held open by a cord threaded through small rings sewn to the back of the curtain, a device known as Italian stringing, or reefing. The pencil pleat heading is made up from a border of the same fabric, cut on the bias and crowned with a bow.

materials & equipment

checked cotton fabric and lining fabric

8 cm (3 in) pencil pleat heading tape

10 cording rings

polyester cord

curtain hooks

2 cm (³⁄₄ in) thick plywood for the pelmet board

angle brackets

metal eyelets

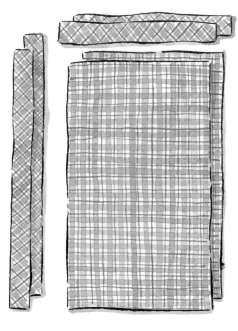

1 Calculate the size of your pelmet board (see Techniques, page 98). It should be 8 cm (3 in) deep. Cut it out and screw eyelets along the front and side edges at 8 cm (3 in) intervals. Attach it to the wall.

2 Measure the window and pelmet board to calculate fabric quantities (see Techniques, page 96). As the curtains have a loose pencil pleat heading, the fabric must be twice the width of the pelmet board, plus 8 cm (3 in) for side hems. Add 24 cm (9½ in) to the length for heading and hem. The border requires two strips of fabric cut on the bias, both 22 cm (9 in) deep, one the same length as the curtain and the other the same length as the width of the curtain. The bow requires four strips of material, two measuring 30 x 60 cm (12 x 24 in) and two 5 x 20 cm (2 x 8 in). The lining is 4 cm (1¾ in) smaller all round than the finished curtain.

3 Cut out the fabric for the curtains and border, joining widths if necessary (see Techniques, page 98). Place the border strips right sides together. At one end, pin and baste the strips together at a 45 degree angle, running down diagonally from the top corner. Check that the angle of the seam is correct and that the checks match up, then machine stitch, stopping 2 cm (¾ in) from the bottom of the strip. Open out the border. Press in a 2 cm (¾ in) fold to the wrong side all around the inner edge.

4 Place the border on top of the curtain, both right sides up, so it runs along the top and outside edge of the curtain. Pin, baste and machine stitch the folded inside edge of the border to the curtain.

5 Turn the curtain over so it is right side down. Press in a 4 cm (1¾ in) hem along the sides and a 8 cm (3 in) double hem at the bottom. Press in the angled mitres (see Techniques, page 100). Pin and baste the hems. Herringbone stitch the side hems and slip stitch the base hem and the mitres.

6 Cut out the lining, joining widths if necessary (see Techniques, page 98). Turn in and press a 2 cm (¾ in) hem along the sides of the lining and a double 2 cm (¾ in) hem along the bottom. Mitre the corners. Pin, baste and machine stitch the side and bottom hems in place.

7 Place the curtain right side down with the lining on top, right side up. Pin the curtain and lining together at the top. Pin, baste and slip stitch the lining to the curtain at the sides. Leave the bottom of the lining open, as the curtain will hang better.

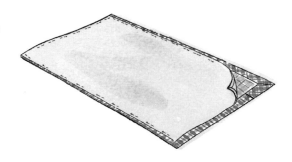

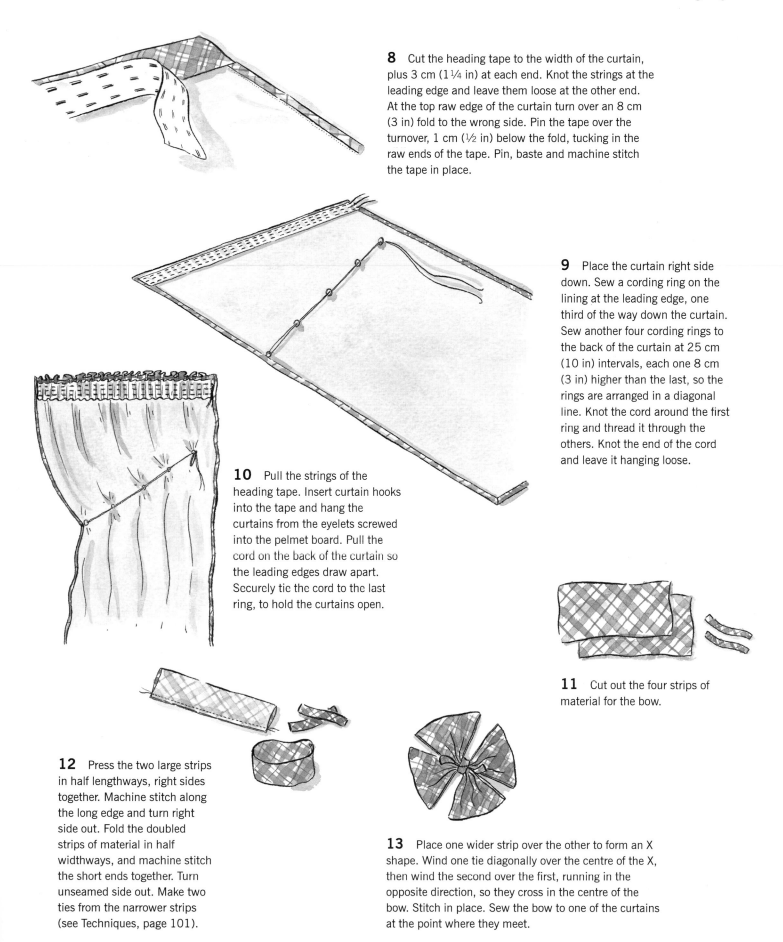

8 Cut the heading tape to the width of the curtain, plus 3 cm (1¼ in) at each end. Knot the strings at the leading edge and leave them loose at the other end. At the top raw edge of the curtain turn over an 8 cm (3 in) fold to the wrong side. Pin the tape over the turnover, 1 cm (½ in) below the fold, tucking in the raw ends of the tape. Pin, baste and machine stitch the tape in place.

9 Place the curtain right side down. Sew a cording ring on the lining at the leading edge, one third of the way down the curtain. Sew another four cording rings to the back of the curtain at 25 cm (10 in) intervals, each one 8 cm (3 in) higher than the last, so the rings are arranged in a diagonal line. Knot the cord around the first ring and thread it through the others. Knot the end of the cord and leave it hanging loose.

10 Pull the strings of the heading tape. Insert curtain hooks into the tape and hang the curtains from the eyelets screwed into the pelmet board. Pull the cord on the back of the curtain so the leading edges draw apart. Securely tie the cord to the last ring, to hold the curtains open.

11 Cut out the four strips of material for the bow.

12 Press the two large strips in half lengthways, right sides together. Machine stitch along the long edge and turn right side out. Fold the doubled strips of material in half widthways, and machine stitch the short ends together. Turn unseamed side out. Make two ties from the narrower strips (see Techniques, page 101).

13 Place one wider strip over the other to form an X shape. Wind one tie diagonally over the centre of the X, then wind the second over the first, running in the opposite direction, so they cross in the centre of the bow. Stitch in place. Sew the bow to one of the curtains at the point where they meet.

squares on squares

Bold borders add a simple yet extremely effective decorative element to a pair of plain cotton curtains. Ideally suited to a small or recessed window, the cheerful checked borders make the curtains into a focal point without swamping the window in folds of fabric. Unobtrusive ties in the same checked fabric as the border hold the curtains to a narrow metal pole with heart-shaped finials that contribute to the overall air of harmonious simplicity.

materials & equipment

heavy cotton fabric
checked cotton for the border and ties

1 To calculate how much fabric you will need, measure the window (see Techniques, page 96). A single width of fabric may be enough for each curtain if you have a small window, but you will have to join widths if your window is larger (see Techniques, page 98). The curtains are self-lined, so the back panel is made from the same fabric as the front panel.

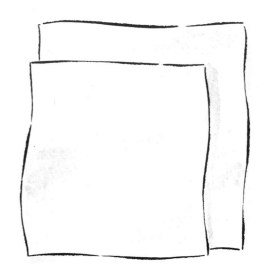

2 The front panel of main fabric for each curtain should be 15 cm (6 in) smaller all round than the back panel, to allow for the border. Cut out the fabric for the front and back panels.

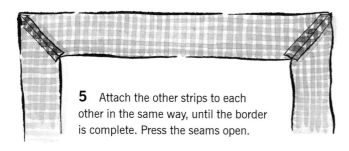

3 For the border cut four strips of fabric, two 20 cm (8 in) deep and the same length as the back panel, and the other two 20 cm (8 in) deep and the same width as the back panel.

4 Place one strip on top of another with right sides together. Pin and baste the strips together at a 45 degree angle from the top corner, stopping 1.5 cm (⅝ in) from the bottom edge. Check that the angle of the join is correct, then machine stitch together. Trim the seams.

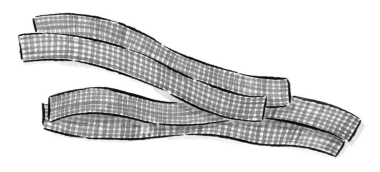

5 Attach the other strips to each other in the same way, until the border is complete. Press the seams open.

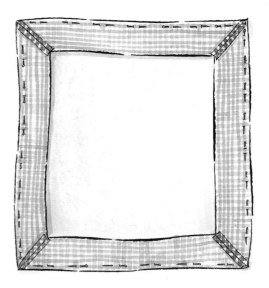

6 Place the back panel on a flat surface, right side up. Place the border on top, right side down. Pin the two together all around the perimeter.

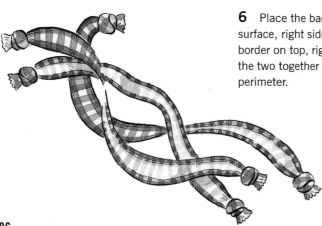

7 You will need one tie every 15 cm (6 in) along the top of the curtain. Cut strips of checked fabric, 4 x 50 cm (1¾ x 20 in). Press in a 5 mm (¼ in) hem all around the edges and machine stitch in place. Knot the ends of each tie.

8 Fold the ties in half widthways and press. Unpin the top of the border and insert the ties between the back panel and the border, placing one tie at each corner and spacing them at regular 15 cm (6 in) intervals in between. Line up the fold of the tie with the raw edge of the curtain, the knotted ends of the ties pointing in towards the centre of the curtain.

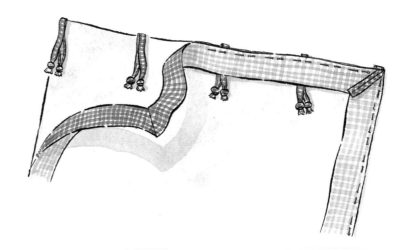

9 When all the ties are in place, baste and machine stitch the back panel and the border together around all four sides, using a 1.5 cm (⅝ in) seam allowance. Take in all the ties as you stitch.

10 Press in a 1.5 cm (⅝ in) hem to the wrong side all around the inside raw edges of the border.

11 Turn the curtain right side out and press. Place it on a flat surface with the border right side up. Slip the front panel into position beneath the border, right side up. The border should overlap the front panel by 2.5 cm (1 in). Pin the border and front panel together all around the inside perimeter of the border.

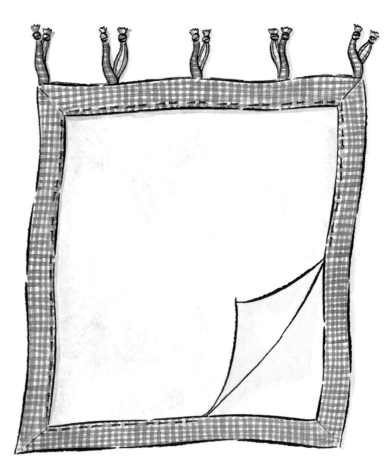

12 Check that the curtain lies flat and smooth before you baste and machine stitch the two layers together from the right side, stitching close to the inside folded edge of the border. Press the curtain and hang it by knotting the ties loosely around a curtain pole.

contrast-scalloped border

An elegant scalloped black felt border provides a striking textural contrast to the crisp, clean folds and snowy white cotton of these floor-length curtains. The border adds definition to the pale curtains and frames the view from the window. The curtains are lined and interlined to give them a luxurious padded thickness.

materials & equipment

white herringbone cotton

interlining

lining fabric

thick black felt

5 cm (2 in) wide pencil pleat heading tape

curtain hooks

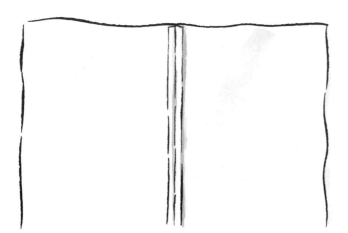

1 To calculate fabric quantities, measure the window (see Techniques, page 96). The curtains have a pencil pleat heading and require fabric two and a half times the length of the pole. Add 16 cm (6½ in) to the length for hem and heading and 12 cm (4¾ in) to the width for side hems. The interlining must be the same size as the curtain without additions for hems. The lining must be 4 cm (1¾ in) smaller than the finished curtain all round. Cut out the main fabric, lining and interlining and join widths (see Techniques, page 98).

2 Make a template for the scalloped border (see Templates, page 103). Cut two strips of felt, each 10 cm (4 in) deep and the same length as the finished curtain. Place the template on top of each strip and mark around it, then cut along the outline.

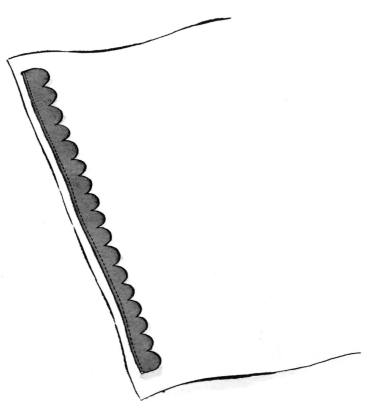

3 Lay the curtain right side up and, using fabric pen, mark a line all the way down one side of the curtain, 6 cm (2½ in) in from the raw edge. Place the straight edge of the felt strip along this line, the scallops sitting on the inside, the top of the strip 8 cm (3 in) below the top of the curtain and the end of the strip 8 cm (3 in) above the bottom of the curtain.

4 Pin, baste and machine stitch the felt to the curtain, 1 cm (½ in) from the straight edge, then zigzag stitch the straight edge of the felt so it lies flat and is unobtrusive.

5 Place the curtain right side down. Use a ruler and fabric pen to mark a series of vertical lines, each 30 cm (12 in) apart, across the back of the curtain.

6 Place the interlining on the curtain, 8 cm (3 in) below the top edge and 8 cm (3 in) above the bottom edge. Fold back the interlining until the fold aligns with the first line then lock stitch the interlining to the curtain (see Techniques, page 99). Continue until the interlining is locked in all the way across the main fabric.

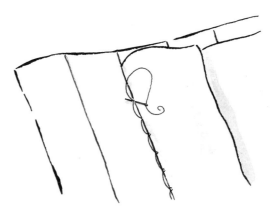

7 Press in a 6 cm (2½ in) hem over the interlining at each side edge of the curtain and a 8 cm (3 in) hem along the bottom edge. Press in the angled mitres (see Techniques, page 100) at the bottom corners of the curtain. The scallops should now sit along the outer edge of the curtain.

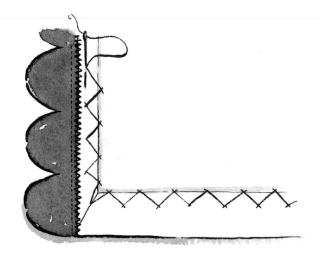

8 Pin and baste the hems. Loosely herringbone stitch the side and base hems and slip stitch the mitres in place.

9 Cut out the lining and join widths if necessary (see Techniques, page 98). Turn in and press a 2 cm (¾ in) fold along the side edges of the lining and a double 2 cm (¾ in) hem along the bottom. Mitre the corners and press. Pin, baste and machine sew the side and bottom hems in place.

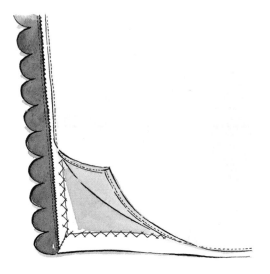

10 Place the curtain on a flat surface, interlined side up. Put the lining on top, right side up. Match up the corners of the lining with the mitred corners of the main fabric and align the top raw edges. There should be a border of fabric showing all round the lining. Pin the lining and curtain together along the top edges. Baste the lining to the curtain, then slip stitch along the folded side edges. Leave the bottom of the lining open, as the curtain will hang better.

11 Cut the heading tape to the width of the curtain plus 3 cm (1¼ in) at each end. Knot the strings at the leading edge and leave them loose at the other. At the top of the curtain, turn in an 8 cm (3 in) fold to the wrong side. Pin the tape over the fold 1 cm (½ in) below the edge, tucking under the raw ends. Pin, baste and machine sew the tape in place. Pull the strings and knot the end. Insert the curtain hooks evenly along the length of the tape and hang the curtains.

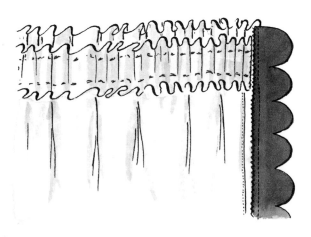

pictorial-edged curtains

An essentially simple pair of curtains has been enlived by the addition of what appears to be a Toile de Jouy undercurtain. In fact the Toile de Jouy is attached to the heavy cream fabric and it is just a deep pleat in the curtain that gives the impression of a separate curtain hanging behind a pair of simple cream drapes.

materials & equipment

plain cotton fabric

Toile de Jouy fabric

lining fabric

2.5 cm (1 in) deep gathering tape

curtain hooks

1 To calculate fabric quantities, measure the window (see Techniques, page 96). The curtains are headed with gathering tape, and require fabric two and a half times the width of the pole or track. Add 12 cm (4¾ in) to the width for side hems and 25 cm (10 in) to the length for hem and heading. Only one width of 135 cm (54 in) Toile de Jouy is necessary for the edging. For the curtains to pool on the floor, add 30 cm (12 in) to the length. The lining must be 4 cm (1¾ in) smaller than the finished curtain all round.

2 Cut out the main fabric and the Toile de Jouy fabric. Cut the length of Toile de Jouy in half (see Techniques, page 98). Join half a width of toile de Jouy to the leading edge of each curtain (see Techniques, page 98).

3 Place the curtain on a flat surface, right side down. Press in a 6 cm (2½ in) hem along the side edges of the fabric and a double 8 cm (3 in) hem at the bottom. Press in the angled mitres at the bottom corners of the curtain (see Techniques, page 100). Pin and baste the hems. Loosely herringbone stitch the side hems in place. Slip stitch the double base hem and the mitres.

4 Cut out the lining fabric and join widths as necessary (see Techniques, page 98). Press in a 2 cm (¾ in) hem along each side edge of the lining and a double 2 cm (¾ in) hem all along the bottom edge. Mitre the corners (see Techniques, page 100). Pin, baste and machine stitch the side and bottom hems in place.

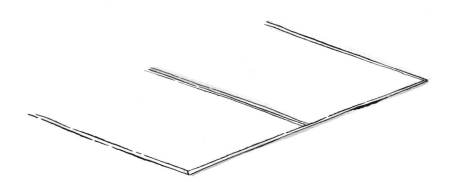

5 Place the curtain on a flat surface, wrong side up. Place the lining on top, right side up. Match up the corners of the lining with the mitred corners of the main fabric and align the top raw edges. A border of main curtain fabric should be showing all around the sides and bottom of the lining.

6 Make sure that the material is lying completely flat before pinning the curtain and the lining together along their top raw edges. Working at the sides of the curtain, pin and baste the lining to the side hems of the curtain. Slip stitch the folded edge of the lining to the curtain. Leave the bottom of the lining open as the curtain will hang better.

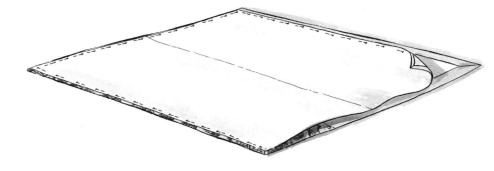

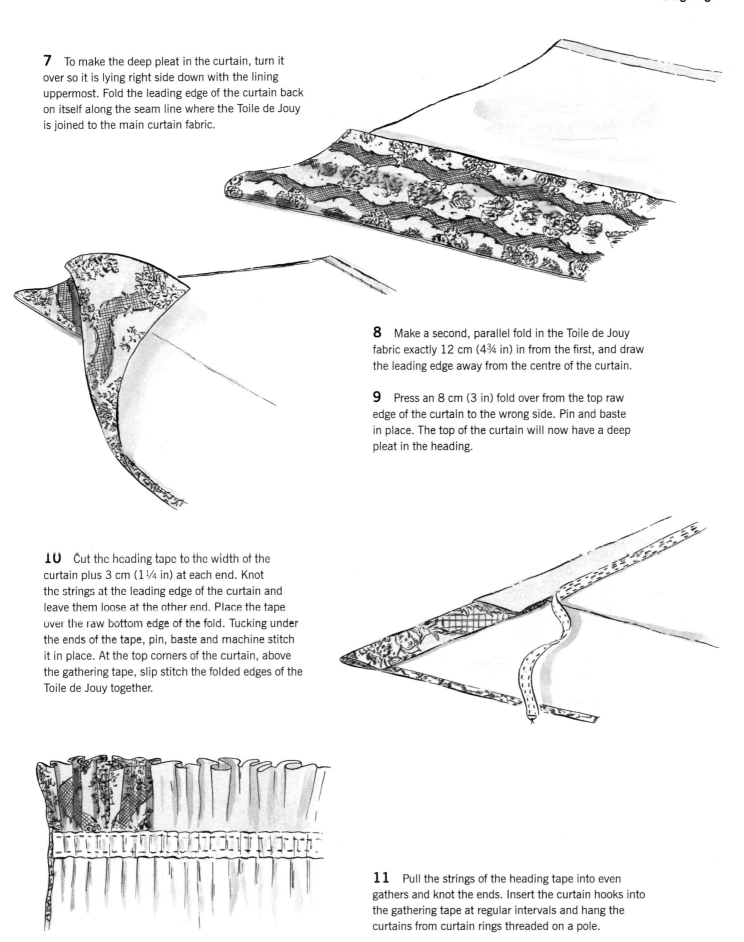

7 To make the deep pleat in the curtain, turn it over so it is lying right side down with the lining uppermost. Fold the leading edge of the curtain back on itself along the seam line where the Toile de Jouy is joined to the main curtain fabric.

8 Make a second, parallel fold in the Toile de Jouy fabric exactly 12 cm (4¾ in) in from the first, and draw the leading edge away from the centre of the curtain.

9 Press an 8 cm (3 in) fold over from the top raw edge of the curtain to the wrong side. Pin and baste in place. The top of the curtain will now have a deep pleat in the heading.

10 Cut the heading tape to the width of the curtain plus 3 cm (1¼ in) at each end. Knot the strings at the leading edge of the curtain and leave them loose at the other end. Place the tape over the raw bottom edge of the fold. Tucking under the ends of the tape, pin, baste and machine stitch it in place. At the top corners of the curtain, above the gathering tape, slip stitch the folded edges of the Toile de Jouy together.

11 Pull the strings of the heading tape into even gathers and knot the ends. Insert the curtain hooks into the gathering tape at regular intervals and hang the curtains from curtain rings threaded on a pole.

equipment and techniques

basic equipment

Anyone planning to make their own curtains will need some basic tools. A pair of good-quality cutting shears is essential, as are a pair of medium-sized dressmaker's scissors and small embroidery scissors for cutting threads. Equally important are a metal tape measure, metre rule and a small plastic ruler, which will enable you to measure up accurately. Use good-quality steel dressmaking pins that will not rust, and store them in a box so they stay sharp. A steam iron is invaluable during the making-up process, but should be used with a damp cloth to protect delicate fabrics. When marking up fabrics, use vanishing fabric pen, which fades to invisibility in 72 hours. A metal thimble is another useful item, as is a knitting needle to coax ties right side out. Some projects in this book involve making a pelmet board from plywood or MDF. To cut the board to the required shape, you will need a jigsaw. Attaching the valance or curtains to the pelmet board may require the use of a staple gun. The projects in this book involve both hand and machine stitches. Basic proficiency in using a sewing machine is necessary, for, although it is possible to make curtains entirely by hand, it is a long and laborious job. Your machine should have a good range of basic stitches. Sophisticated accessories are not needed, but a piping foot is required for some of the projects in this book. Finally, the process of making curtains will be easier and more enjoyable if you work in a well-ventilated and well-lit spot and have access to a large worktable.

choosing fabric

For each project the fabrics are specified, as the weight, texture and pattern is suited to the particular design. If you want to use an alternative material, select fabric of a similar weight. Always check that your chosen fabric is preshrunk and fade-resistant. Before you cut into the fabric, examine it for any flaws. Minor flaws can sometimes be incorporated into the hem or heading. If the fabric is badly flawed, return it to the retailer or manufacturer. The fire-retardant qualities of furnishing fabrics are governed by legislation in most countries. We suggest that you obtain advice from the manufacturer of your chosen fabric or a specialist furnishing fabrics retailer. Cleaning instructions are printed on the selvedges of most fabrics in the form of care symbols. Any lined or interlined items must always be dry cleaned.

measuring the window

Before starting to make curtains, you must accurately measure the window to calculate how much fabric you will need. This is a very important calculation, so take your time and carefully check your measurements over again once you have finished. If possible, fix the track, pole or pelmet board in place before measuring the window. The track or pole should be attached about 5–15 cm (2–6 in) above the window frame, with the ends projecting at least 10 cm (4 in) beyond the sides of the window. Take measurements with a steel tape measure. If the window is particularly tall or wide, enlist the help of an assistant.

The two measurements needed in order to calculate fabric quantities for a pair of curtains are the width and the length of the window. To work out the width of the finished curtains, measure the width of the track, rail or pole (not the window). If you are using a pelmet board, measure the sides and front. To calculate the drop of finished full-length curtains, measure from the top of the track or bottom of the pole down to the floor. For sill-length curtains, measure from the top of the track or bottom of the pole down to the sill. For apron-length curtains measure from the top of the track or pole to just below the sill or to the desired point.

calculating fabric quantities

Length

The drop from the pole, track or rail to the floor, sill or other desired point will determine the length of the finished curtains. Add the appropriate heading and hem allowances (given in the individual projects).

Width

The amount of fabric required is dictated by the curtain heading. Pencil pleat heading tape, for example, requires fabric that is two and a half times as wide as the pole or track. Add the allowances for hems and joining widths (given in the individual projects).

To calculate how much fabric you will need:

1. Multiply the length of the pole or track by the heading requirement (2.5 for pencil pleat heading) to reach the final fabric width.
E.g. Length of the track or pole = 200 cm (6 ft)
    Pencil pleat heading = 2.5 x length
    Width of fabric = 200 x 2.5 = 500 cm (15 ft)

2. Divide this measurement by the width of your fabric to calculate how many widths of fabric are required. Round up the final figure to the next full width.
E.g. Width of chosen fabric = 135 cm (54 in)
    Width of fabric needed = 500 cm
    500 divided by 135 cm = 3.7
    Rounds up to 4

3. Multiply this figure by the unfinished length of the curtain to find out how much fabric is needed.
E.g. Working drop = 300 cm (10 ft)
    300 x 4 = 1200
Therefore, the total length of fabric required is 12 m (40 ft), 6 m (20 ft) for each curtain.

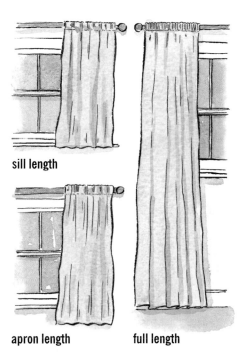

sill length

apron length   **full length**

allowing for pattern repeats

If you are using patterned fabric, you will need extra fabric in the length in order to match the pattern across the curtains. To match the pattern, you need to know the length of the pattern repeat (the fabric supplier will be able to provide you with this information). Divide the unfinished length of each curtain by the length of the repeat, round up the result to the next full figure, then multiply it by the length of the repeat to find out how much fabric you will need.

    E.g. The unfinished length of your curtain (including allowances) is 400 cm (12½ ft)
    The pattern repeat is 90 cm (36 in)
    400 divided by 90 = 4.44
    Rounded up to 5
    5 multiplied by 90 = 450
    Each cut length must be 450 cm (113½ ft) long.

heading requirements

A few standard heading requirements:

gathering tape

2–2½ times length of track

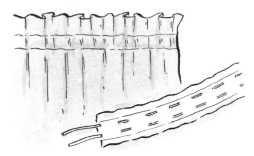

pencil pleat tape

2½–3 times length of track

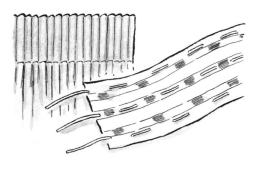

ties

1–2 times length of track

cased heading

2–3 times length of track

cutting out the fabric

It is essential that the fabric is cut straight, or the curtain will hang crooked. Place the fabric on a flat surface. Use a metal ruler and set square to mark a straight line in pencil or fabric pen on the wrong side of the fabric. Cut along the line. To cut a width in half, fold it selvedge to selvedge and cut along the fold. If you are using fabric with a high pile, mark the top of each width with a notch so all the fabric will run in the right direction on the finished curtain.

joining widths

Always place any half widths at the outside edge of the curtain, with a full width at the leading edge. To join two widths, place them right sides together, aligning the raw edges that are to be seamed, and pin, baste and machine stitch a straight seam 1.5 cm (⅝ in) from the raw edges. Trim away any surplus material. If the fabric puckers, clip the seams so the cloth lies flat.

matching patterns across joined widths

Fold under a 1.5 cm (⅝ in) seam allowance on one width of the patterned fabric and press. Lay out the other piece of patterned fabric, right side up, on a flat surface. Place the fabric with the folded edge on the second piece of fabric and match the pattern. Pin in place across the fold.

calculating the size of a pelmet board

The pelmet board should be approximately 12–18 cm (5–7 in) deep, so that the curtains project far enough beyond the window. It must be the width of the window frame plus 10 cm (4 in) to give clearance at each end.

making a pelmet board

Cut the plywood or MDF to the required proportions and sand any rough edges. Attach a pair of angled brackets to the underside of the board. This is now the back edge. Two brackets will support a short board; use three or four brackets if you have a long or heavy board. If the pelmet board is visible behind the curtains, it must be covered. Cut a piece of matching fabric that is large enough to cover the board, lay it flat, wrong side up, and place the board in the centre. Fold the fabric over the board and staple it in place.

basic sewing techniques

basting stitch

This temporary stitch holds fabric in place until it is permanently stitched. Use a colourful thread so the basting is clearly visible and therefore easy to remove.

slip stitch

Slip stitch holds a folded edge to flat fabric or two folded edges together, as in a mitred corner. Work on the wrong side of the fabric from right to left. Start with the needle in the fold. Push it out and pick up a few threads from the flat fabric, then insert it into the hem again, all in one smooth and continuous movement. When finished, the stitches should be almost invisible.

herringbone stitch

This stitch is used to hold a raw edge to flat fabric. Work from left to right with the needle pointing from right to left. Starting in the fold, bring the needle through the hem at a 45 degree angle. Take a stitch in the single layer of fabric, approximately 5 mm (1/4 in) above the hem, picking up a couple of threads. Bring the needle diagonally down to the hem and make a small backward stitch through one thickness of fabric. Keep the stitches loose.

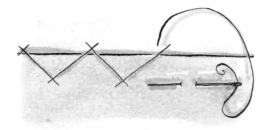

lock stitch

This stitch holds interlining or lining and fabric together. It is a loose stitch, allowing some movement between the layers. It is worked from the bottom of the curtain to the top. Fold back the interlining and make a stitch through the folded interlining and main fabric, picking up only a couple of threads with each stitch. Make the next stitch about 5 cm (2 in) further up the interlining. Keep the stitches very slack.

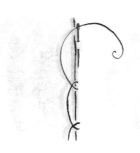

buttonhole stitch

This is used for buttonholes or wherever a raw edge needs to be strengthened or neatened. Work from left to right with the raw edge uppermost. Push the needle through the fabric from back to front, approximately 3 mm (1/8 in) below the raw edge. Twist the thread around the tip of the needle, then pull the needle through to form a knot at the raw edge of the fabric.

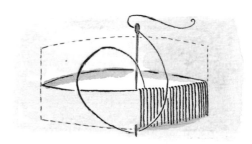

flat seam

This seam is used to join pieces of fabric. Place the two pieces of fabric right sides together, aligning the edges that are to be seamed. Pin and baste, then machine sew the seam. Reverse the stitches at the beginning and end of the seam to secure it in place.

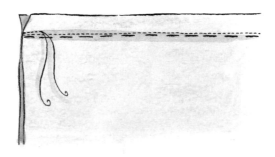

flat fell seam

This sturdy seam is designed for heavy fabric. Pin the fabrics right sides together and baste along the seam line. Machine stitch the seam. Press it open and then over to one side. Trim the underneath seam to half its width. Fold the upper seam allowance over the trimmed one and baste. Machine stitch in place close to the folded edge.

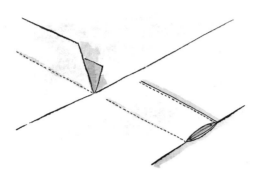

french seam

This self-neatening seam contains all raw edges and is used for sheers and lightweight fabrics. Place two pieces of fabric wrong sides together, aligning the raw edges that are to be seamed. Pin, baste and machine stitch a seam close to the raw edge. Trim the seam. Fold the material right sides together and pin, baste and machine stitch a second seam 1 cm (½ in) from the first, enclosing the raw edges in a narrow tube of fabric.

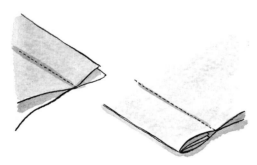

double base hem

Most curtains are finished at the bottom with a double base hem, which encloses any raw edges and lies flat against the back of the curtain. The base hem on lining is also usually finished with a double hem. For a 10 cm (4 in) double hem, the hem allowance is 20 cm (8 in). Press up the hem allowance along the bottom edge of the curtain. Open out the hem, then fold the raw edge up to the pressed line. Fold up again and stitch in place.

mitring corners

Mitring is the neatest way of working hem corners. Press in the required hem allowance along the bottom and sides of the fabric, then open them out flat again. Where the two fold lines meet, make

a 45 degree fold in the fabric and press in place. Turn in the hems along the pressed folds. The edges of the hems will form a neat diagonal line at the corner. Use slip stitch to secure the mitre.

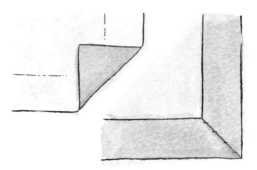

making an angled mitre

An angled mitre is necessary when a bottom hem is wider than the side hems. Press in the hem allowance along the bottom and sides of the fabric, then open out again. Fold in the corner of the fabric towards the bottom hem of the curtain. Then make the first fold in the double hem. Fold in the side hem, then make the second fold in the double hem. The folded edges should meet.

making ties and tabs

As an alternative to hooks and heading tape, curtains can be attached to a pole or rail with ties. To make a tie, cut a strip of material to the desired width and length. Fold the strip in half along the length, right sides together. Pin, baste and machine sew along the long end and one short end, leaving the other end unstitched. Turn the tie right side out with the aid of a knitting needle. Press a 5 mm (¼ in) fold to the inside of the tie and slip stitch the end closed. The heavier the curtain, the wider the tie should be. Tabs are made in exactly the same way as ties; the only difference is that the strip of fabric is wider.

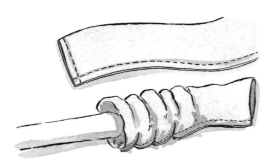

making bias binding

Bias binding is an effective and attractive way to enclose raw edges of fabric. It is available ready made but it is easy to make. Place your chosen fabric on a flat surface, wrong side up. Diagonally fold in one corner until the end of the fabric is aligned with the selvedge, forming a triangle of fabric. The diagonal fold line is the bias line of the material. Mark strips parallel to the bias line all the way across the fabric, then cut them out.

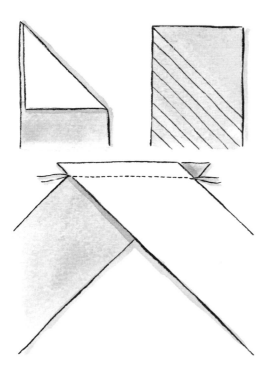

Join the strips to make a continuous strip of bias binding. Place two strips right sides together at right angles, lining up the raw edges. Pin and machine stitch together, using a 5 mm (¼ in) seam allowance. Trim the seams, press flat and trim the corners.

making piping

Piping is made from a length of cord covered with bias binding. The binding must be wide enough to cover the cord and to allow a 1.5 cm (⅝ in) seam allowance either side of it. Wrap the binding around the cord, then baste and machine stitch close to the cord, using a piping foot.

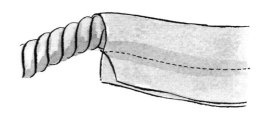

making box pleats

Box pleats give a tailored finish to curtains and valances. One box pleat requires fabric three times the width of the pleat. Decide on the finished width of each pleat and multiply it by three. The finished width of the object you are making must be divisible by this measurement. For example, if each pleat is 10 cm (4 in) wide, the width of the item to be pleated must be exactly divisible by 30 cm (12 in). If it is not, adjust either the width of the object or the width of the pleat. For a 10 cm (4 in) pleat, mark a fold 5 cm (2 in) from the edge of the fabric and another 5 cm (2 in) from that. Then mark alternate 10 cm (4 in) and 5 cm (2 in) folds across the top of the fabric. Fold along the first mark, 5 cm (2 in) from the edge of the curtain, and bring it across to join a mark 20 cm (8 in) on from it. Pin the folds together. Leave a 10 cm (4 in) space and repeat the action all the way across the width of the fabric.

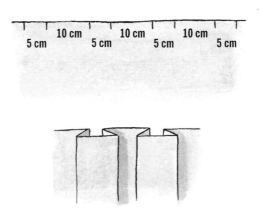

templates

All the templates in this book must be enlarged. Either use a photocopier to enlarge the template to the desired proportions (sometimes stated in the individual project) on stiff paper or cardboard, or trace the pattern on to graph paper, increase the proportions to the desired size, then trace on to stiff paper or cardboard. Cut out the template. Pin it to the wrong side of your fabric, then mark all the way around the outline of the template in fabric pen.

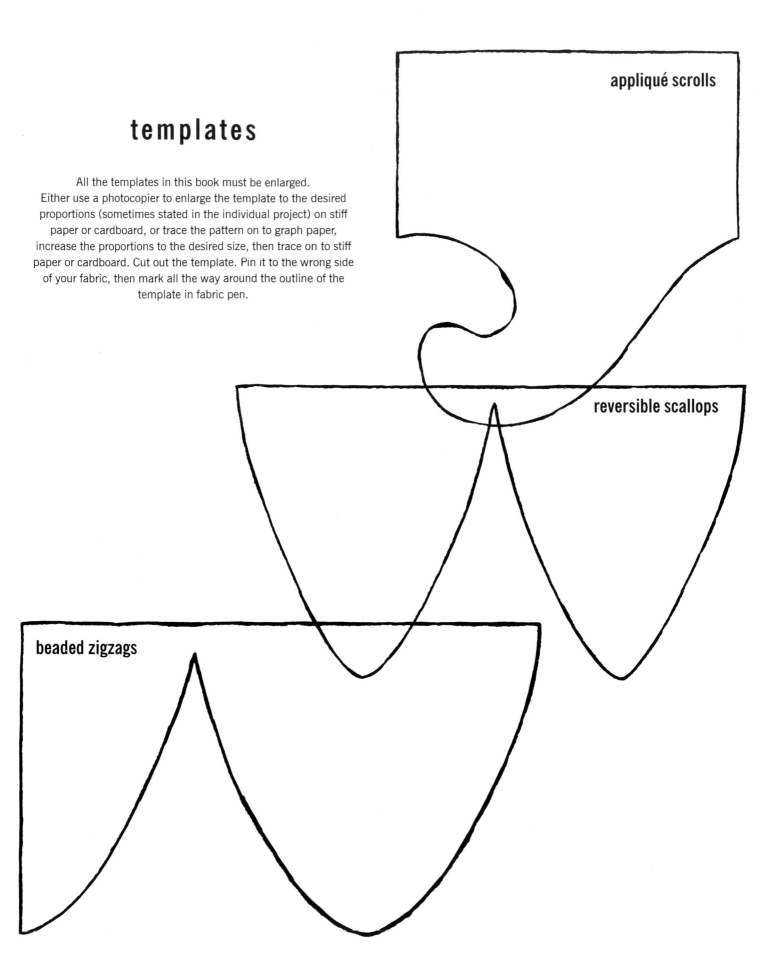

appliqué scrolls

reversible scallops

beaded zigzags

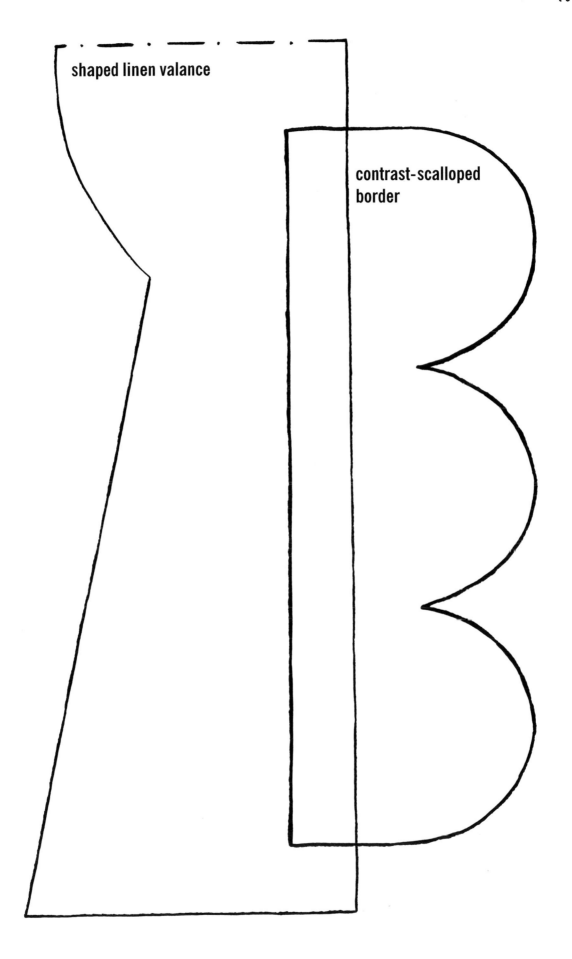

shaped linen valance

contrast-scalloped
border

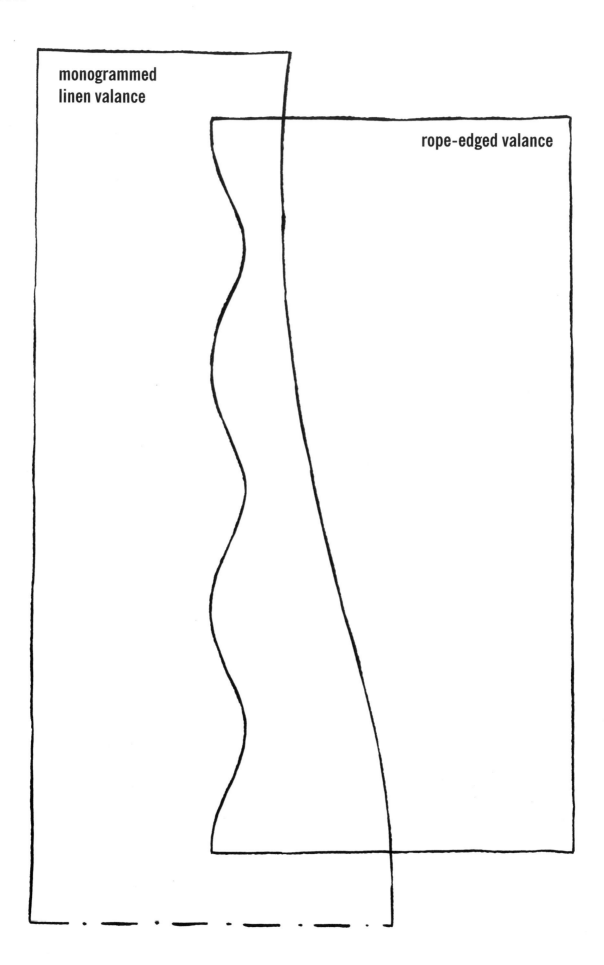

monogrammed
linen valance

rope-edged valance

directory of suppliers

Fabrics

Abbott & Boyd
1/22 Chelsea Harbour Design
 Centre
London SW10 0XE
Tel: 020 7351 9985
www.abbottandboyd.co.uk

Anta
Fearn
Tain
Ross-shire
Scotland IV20 1XW
Tel: 01862 832 477
www.anta.com

Baer & Ingram
Dragon Works
Leigh-on-Mendip
Radstock
Somerset BA3 5QZ
Tel: 01373 813 800
www.baer-ingram.com

B. Brown-Muraspec
Zoffany House
74–78 Wood Lane End
Hemel Hempstead
Hertfordshire HP2 4RF
Tel: 0870 5117 118
www.muraspec.co.uk

Cath Kidston
51 Marylebone High Street
London W1U 5HW
Tel: 020 7935 6555
www.cathkidston.co.uk

Celia Birtwell
71 Westbourne Park Road
London W2 5QH
Tel: 020 7221 0877

Colefax & Fowler
110 Fulham Road
London SW3 6XL
Tel: 020 7244 7427

Designers Guild
277 King's Road
London SW3 5EN
Tel: 020 7243 7300
www.designersguild.com

Fabrics Galore
52–54 Lavender Hill
London SW11 5RH
Tel: 020 7738 9589

GP & J Baker
Unit 18–19 Chelsea Harbour
 Design Centre
London SW10 0XE
Tel: 020 7351 7760
www.gpjbaker.co.uk

Ian Mankin
109 Regent's Park Road
London NW1 8UR
Tel: 020 7722 0997

Ian Sanderson
Chelsea Harbour Design
 Centre
London SW10 0XE
Tel: 020 7352 6919

Ikea
www.ikea.com

JAB International
Chelsea Harbour Design
 Centre
London SW10 0XE
Tel: 020 7349 9323
www.jab.de

Jane Churchill
110 Fulham Road
London SW3 6RL
Tel: 020 7244 7427

John Lewis
www.johnlewis.com

KA International
68 Sloane Street
London SW3 3DD
Tel: 020 7503 3200
www.ka-international.com

Laura Ashley
Freepost
PO Box 5
Newton
Powys SY16 1LX
Tel: 0800 868100
www.lauraashley.com

Manuel Canovas
110 Fulham Road
London SW3 6RL
Tel: 020 7244 7427

Nicole Fabre
592 King's Road
London SW6 2DX
Tel: 020 7384 3112

Nya Nordiska
2/26 Chelsea Harbour Design
   Centre
London SW10 OXE
Tel: 020 7351 2783
www.nya-nordiska.com

Osborne & Little
304 King's Road
London SW3 5UH
Tel: 020 7352 1456
www.osborneandlittle.com

Pierre Frey
251–253 Fulham Road
London SW3 6HY
Tel: 020 7376 5599
www.pierrefrey.fr

Sanderson
233 King's Road
London SW3 5EJ
Tel: 020 7351 7728
www.sanderson-online.co.uk

Sahco Hesslein
G24 Chelsea Harbour Design Centre
London SW10 OXE
Tel: 020 7352 6168
www.sahco-hesslein.com

Shaker
Tel: 020 7935 9461
www.shaker.co.uk

Streets
Frederick House
Hurricane Way
Wickford Business Park
Wickford
Essex SF11 8YB
Tel: 01268 766677
www.streets.co.uk

Tobias & the Angel
68 White Hart Lane
Barnes
London SW13 OPZ
Tel: 020 8878 8902

V.V. Rouleaux
54 Sloane Square
Clivedon Place
London SW1W 8AX
Tel: 020 7730 3125
www.vvrouleaux.com

Curtainalia

The Bradley Collection
Lion Barn
Maitland Road
Needham Market
Suffolk IP6 8N
Tel: 01449 722724
www.bradleycollection.co.uk

Byron & Byron
10 Stouer Road
London E3 2NT
Tel: 020 8510 4800

Cameron Fuller
Unit 1–3
Weston Park
Devonshire Way
Honiton EX14 1ST
Tel: 01404 47568
www.cameronfuller.co.uk

Cope & Timmins
Angel Road Works
Angel Road
London N18 3AH
Tel: 0845 458 8861
www.copes.co.uk

Hallis Hudson
Redscar Industrial Estate
Unit B1
Longridge Road
Preston
Lancashire PR2 5NJ
Tel: 01722 202202
www.hallishudson.com

McKinney & Co
The Old Imperial Laundry
71 Warriner Gardens
London SW11 4XW
Tel: 020 7627 5088

Nordic Style
109 Lots Road
London SW10 ORN
Tel: 020 7351 1755
www.nordicstyle.com

John Lewis
Tel: 08456 049049
www.johnlewis.com

Silent Gliss
Star Lane
Margate
Kent CT9 4EF
Tel: 01843 863571
www.silentgliss.com

Walcot House
Lyneham Heath Studios
Lyneham
Chipping Norton
Oxfordshire OX7 6QQ
Tel: 01993 832940
www.walcothouse.com

credits

page 1 antique fabric
page 2 fabrics from Sanderson, pole from Byron & Byron
page 4 above from left to right: plain fabric from Sanderson, checked fabric from KA International; fabric from Sanderson, tension wire kit from Ikea; below: fabric from Streets
page 5 from left to right: both fabrics from KA International; antique fabric
page 7 ready-made curtains from Habitat

use of fabrics *pages 8–9*
1 antique curtains
2 fabric, fringe and pole from John Lewis
3 antique fabric
4 ready-made curtains from Habitat
5 fabric from Osborne & Little, pole and brackets from Byron & Byron
6 Toile de Jouy from Christopher Moore Textiles, pole from McKinney & Co
7 ready-made curtains from Habitat

projects: yellow checks: fabrics from Ian Mankin, trimmings from V. V. Rouleaux • horizontal stripes: fabrics from Sanderson, poles, brackets and rings from Byron & Byron • two-way striped voile: antique fabric • appliqué scrolls: fabrics from Sanderson, pole and brackets from Byron & Byron • contrast-bordered linen: linen from Nicole Fabre, curtains by Reed Creative Services

headings *pages 30–31*
1 antique voile and fixtures
2 fabric from Streets, pole from Hallis Hudson
3 antique linen, pole and brackets from McKinney & Co
4 fabric from Jane Churchill, pole from McKinney & Co
5 fabric from Ian Mankin, pole and rings from John Lewis
6 vintage fabric, poles from Hallis Hudson, antique ring clips from McKinney & Co
7 fabric from Habitat, pole from McKinney & Co
8 fabric from Shaker, pole from Bradley
9 fabric from Sanderson, pole from Byron & Byron
10 fabric from Ian Mankin
11 fabric from Nordic Style
12 fabric, pole and fringe from John Lewis fabric from Ian Mankin

projects: reversible scallops: fabric from Pierre Frey • button-on silk: fabric from Pongees, ammonite knobs from John Lewis • concertina stripes: fabric from Sanderson, tension wire kit from Ikea • tie-on muslin sheers: muslin from JAB, pole made to order

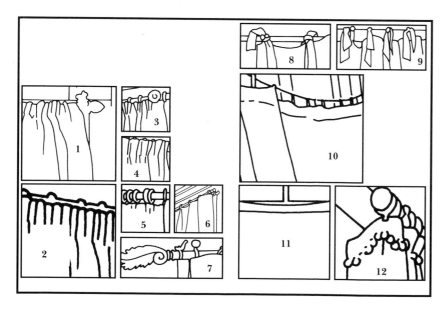

valances and pelmets *pages 48–49*

1   fabric from Jane Churchill
2   fabric from Shaker
3   fabric from John Lewis
4   fabric from Colefax & Fowler
5   fabric from Baer & Ingram
6   fabric from Colefax & Fowler
7   large checked fabric from Laura Ashley, sheer checked fabric from John Lewis

projects: gathered gingham: fabric from John Lewis • monogrammed linen valance: fabric from Streets • beaded zigzags: fabric from Ian Sanderson, beads from John Lewis • red-trimmed voile: fabric from Sanderson, binding from John Lewis • shaped linen valance: fabric from Sahco Hesslein • rope-edged valance: fabric from Designers Guild, rope trim from V. V. Rouleaux • gypsy-skirted valance: vintage fabric, glass beads from V. V. Rouleaux

edgings *pages 78–79*

1–2 fabric from John Lewis, fringe from V. V. Rouleaux
3   sheer fabric from Sanderson, ribbon from V. V. Rouleaux, expansion rod from John Lewis
4   fabrics from John Lewis
5   fabric from Sanderson, fringe from V. V. Rouleaux
6–7 fabric and bobble fringe from Jane Churchill
8   striped fabric from Streets, checked fabric from John Lewis
9   fabric and fringe from John Lewis
10   vintage fabric

page 96   ready-made curtains from Habitat
page 105   antique curtains
page 106   fabric from Designers Guild, rope trimming from V. V. Rouleaux
page 110   fabric from Ian Mankin, trimming from V. V. Rouleaux
page 111   fabric from Baer & Ingram
page 112   fabric from Shaker
endpapers: fabric from Designers Guild, rope trim from V. V. Rouleaux

projects: Italian stringing with bow: fabric from Jane Churchill • squares on squares: plain fabric from Sanderson, checked fabric from KA International • contrast-scalloped border: fabric from Streets, felt from B. Brown, pole from Hallis Hudson • pictorial-edged curtains: both fabrics from KA International

glossary

Appliqué
Applying a second layer of fabric to a main fabric, usually with decorative stitching.

Bias binding
A strip of cloth cut on the bias, at 45 degree to the selvedge, which gives stretch to the fabric. Used as edging or to cover piping cord.

Box pleat
A flat symmetrical pleat formed by folding the fabric to the back at each side of the pleat.

Braid
A woven ribbon used as edging or trimming.

Buckram
Hessian, or another coarse cloth, stiffened with size and used to give rigidity to pelmets.

Cased heading
A simple curtain heading in which a sleeve of material is left open at the top of the curtain to receive a curtain rod or pole.

Cotton
A natural fabric, made from the boll of the cotton plant.

Eyelet
A metal ring punched through fabric to create a bound hole through which poles, rods or wire can be inserted.

Felt
Unwoven cloth made from pounded wool. The edges do not fray after cutting.

Finial
A decorative fixture attached to each end of a curtain pole to hold the curtains on the pole.

Gathering tape
A heading tape that creates an informal shallow, ruffled effect.

Gingham
A plain-weave cotton cloth with a checked pattern.

Heading
The top of a curtain, finished with tape, ties, rings or other treatments.

Heading tape
Ready-made tape that is attached to the top of a curtain to create a particular heading.

Hessian
A strong, coarse fabric made from jute or hemp fibres.

Interlining
A soft material inserted between fabric and lining that provides insulation and gives the curtains a luxurious padded quality.

Italian stringing
A method of drawing curtains with a fixed heading that is kept permanently closed. Cord is threaded through rings on the back of the curtain, then pulled to draw the leading edges apart.

Laminate
A thin protective covering, bonded to a material.

Leading edge
The inside edges of a pair of curtains.

Lining fabric
A secondary fabric used to back curtains and protect them from light and dust. Usually a cotton sateen fabric with a slight sheen.

Mitre
The diagonal join of two pieces of fabric formed at a corner.

Muslin
A sheer, strong woven fabric.

Pelmet
A stiffened piece of fabric that is glued, nailed or hung from a pelmet board positioned above the window.

Pencil pleat heading
A popular heading tape that creates regular, stiff pleats.

Piping
A length of cord covered with bias binding, used as a decorative edging.

Pleat
A fold or crease, pressed or stitched in place.

Raw edge
The cut edge of fabric, without selvedge or hem.

Seam allowance
The narrow strip of raw-edged fabric left to either side of a stitched seam.

Selvedge
Defined warp edge of the fabric, woven to prevent unravelling.

Sheers
Fine, translucent fabrics such as muslin and voile that filter daylight while preserving privacy.

Silk
A luxurious and soft, yet strong, fabric produced by silkworms.

Ticking
A striped, closely woven heavy cotton twill fabric.

Toile de Jouy
A cotton cloth printed with pastoral scenes in a single colour on a neutral background.

Valance
A strip of fabric that runs across the top of a window or around the base of a bed.

Voile
A light plain-weave cotton or man-made fabric.

Width
The distance from selvedge to selvedge on any fabric.

index

basting stitch, 99
bias binding, 32 35, 48, 62 65, 101, 110
  making, 101
  borders, 26–29, 49, 66–69, 74–77, 79, 84–87, 88–91, 103
box pleats, 48, 57, 110
  making, 101
brackets, angled, 48, 54, 57, 74, 80, 98
buckram, 48, 110
buttonhole stitch, 99
buttonholes, 39
buttons, 36, 38, 39

chenille, 31
chintz, 22
cord, piping, 58, 60, 101
cord, polyester, 80
cording rings, 80, 83
cotton, 8, 9, 14, 22, 40, 49, 58, 66, 70, 74, 79, 84, 88, 92, 110
curtain hooks, 14, 17, 18, 21, 29, 30, 58, 61, 74, 77, 80, 83, 88, 91, 92, 95
curtain poles, 9, 10, 13, 14, 25, 30, 31, 32, 35, 44, 46, 47, 60, 61, 64, 65, 66, 68, 69, 73, 84, 87, 94, 96, 97
curtain rails, 30, 97
curtain rings, 29, 30
  clip-on, 30, 32, 35, 62, 65
curtain rods, 50–53, 66
curtain track, 29, 30, 48, 96, 97, 98
curtain wire, 50, 53

edgings, 78–79, 80–83, 84–87, 88 91, 92 95
embroidery, 56
eyelets, metal, 18, 21, 40, 43, 74, 76, 77, 80, 82, 83, 110

fabric
  calculating quantities, 97
  choosing, 96
  cutting out, 98
fabric glue, 40, 43
fabric pens, 96, 98
felt, 88, 90, 110
finials, 14, 30, 66, 69, 84, 110
fringing
  bobble, 8, 31, 79
  silk, 78
  tassel, 44–47, 78, 79

gingham, 48, 49, 50–53, 58, 78, 110

heading strips, 18, 20, 21, 25, 58
heading tape, 14–17, 26–29, 30 31, 49, 58–61, 74–77, 80–83, 88–91, 92–95, 97, 98, 110
  gathering tape, 30, 48, 58, 60, 92, 94, 95, 98, 110
  pencil pleat, 27, 28, 30, 74, 76, 77, 80, 82, 83, 88, 90, 97, 98, 110
  pinch pleat, 14, 17, 30
headings, 30–31, 32–35, 36–39, 40–42, 44–47
  cased, 30, 31, 48, 50–53, 66–69, 98

tab, 9, 36, 38, 39
tic, 10, 22 25, 30 31, 44 47, 70–72, 84–87
hem, double base, 21, 28, 39, 47, 53, 65, 77, 83, 91, 94, 100
herringbone stitch, 99
hessian, 22, 24, 48, 110
hole punch kit, 18, 21, 40, 43

interfacing, 40, 42
interlining, 8, 14, 16, 17, 74, 76, 77, 88, 90, 91, 96, 110

jigsaw, 96, 98

knitting needle, 96

leading edge, 9, 28, 47, 49, 78, 79, 82, 83, 91, 94, 95, 110
linen, 26–29, 48, 54–57, 66–69
lining, 8, 10, 12, 13, 14, 16, 17, 28, 56, 57, 58, 60, 74, 76, 77, 80, 82, 88, 92, 94, 96, 110
lock stitch, 99

MDF, 96, 98
metre rule, 96
mitres, angled, 100
mitring corners, 100
muslin, 9, 44–47, 110

pattern repeats, 97
pelmet boards, 48, 49, 54, 56, 57, 76, 77, 80, 82, 83, 96, 97
  calculating the size of, 98
  making, 98
pelmets, 6, 48–49, 70–73, 104, 110
piping cord, 58–61, 110
  making, 101

piping foot, 60, 96, 101
pleats, 56, 92, 95, 110
plywood, 54, 74, 80, 96, 98

scalloping, 32–35, 49, 78, 88–91
seams
  flat, 99
  flat fell, 100
  French, 100
set square, 98
sewing machine, 96
slip stitch, 99
staple gun, 54, 57, 96
stapling, 48, 57
steam iron, 96

tape measure, 96
templates, 24, 34, 56, 60, 68, 72, 102–104, 110
tension wire, 40, 43
thimble, 96
tie-backs, metal, 36, 39, 62
ties, 10–13, 22–25, 30–31, 44–47, 70–73, 81–83, 84–87, 98
  making, 101
Toile de Jouy, 8, 9, 92–95, 110

valances, 32, 34, 35, 48, 49, 50–53, 54–57, 58–61, 62–64, 66–68, 74–76, 110
voile, 9, 18–21, 30, 48, 62–65, 78, 79, 110

widths, joining 98
  matching patterns across, 98

zigzag stitch, 42, 57, 65, 69, 89

acknowledgments

Many thanks to all the fabric companies and their public relations staff who so generously gave us yards and yards of fabric to make up the curtains for this book. They include Jane Churchill, Designers Guild, Pierre Frey, KA International, Ian Mankin, Osborne & Little, Sahco Hesslein, Sanderson and Shaker. Thanks also to Tim Leese and Bobby Chance, Liz Shirley, Susie Tinsley and Fiona Wheeler for kindly allowing us to invade their houses and festoon every window with curtains to photograph. Hänsi Schneider has made most of the curtains in this book with her usual superb skill and talent. Many thanks always. Helena Lynch also made some of the curtains — brilliantly. James Merrell has taken superb photographs of a difficult subject with his usual calm control. Thank you to Michael Hill for his wonderful illustrations and to all at Ryland Peters & Small for another good team effort. Finally, many thanks to Catherine Coombes, for her huge hard work, both on this book and at home.

dedication

For Janey Joicey-Cecil, a true and loving friend, with gratitude.